A TOUGH ROW TO HOE:

The 1985 Farm Bill and Beyond

William A. Galston

A TOUGH ROW TO HOE:

The 1985 Farm Bill and Beyond

By

William A. Galston

The Food and Agriculture Policy Project
Susan E. Sechler, Director
Roosevelt Center for American Policy Studies
316 Pennsylvania Avenue, S.E., Suite 500, Washington, D.C. 20003
250 South Wacker Drive, Suite 1250, Chicago, Illinois 60606

HAMILTON
PRESS
LANHAM • NEW YORK • LONDON

Roosevelt Center for
American Policy Studies

Copyright © 1985 by

Roosevelt Center for American Policy Studies

Hamilton Press

4720 Boston Way
Lanham, MD 20706

3 Henrietta Street
London WC2E 8LU England

Printed in the United States of America

ISBN 0-8191-4805-9

Co-published by arrangement with the
Roosevelt Center for American Policy Studies

HAMILTON
PRESS
LANHAM • NEW YORK • LONDON

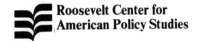 Roosevelt Center for
American Policy Studies

Board of Trustees

Founded in 1982, the Roosevelt Center takes its name and inspiration from three Roosevelts—Theodore, Eleanor, and Franklin—who courageously addressed our nation's future and brought clarity to America's vision of itself.

The Roosevelt Center is a nonprofit, nonpartisan public policy research institute with offices in Washington, D.C., and Chicago. Its goals are to clarify the policy choices before the nation and to encourage the participation of citizens in the decision-making process at all levels of government. The Center's program develops a comprehensive range of reasoned options and strategies concerning critical policy issues facing the United States. The Center does not advocate particular policy alternatives, in the belief that the genius of our political system springs from a free market in ideas.

The Roosevelt Center is dedicated to increasing public awareness of critical policy issues. To that end, it devotes a substantial part of its resources to developing and marketing a family of policy products, including policy options papers, citizens guides, policy road maps, scholarly publications, op-ed pieces, editorial advisories, conference reports, "The American Debate" television series, and videotapes on selected policy issues.

Contents

Preface

The Food and Agriculture Project of the Roosevelt Center was conceived early in 1984 in response to a set of economic and political conditions which, if continued unabated, would lead to a major transformation of the entire U. S. agricultural system. In keeping with the Center's overall mission, the purpose of the project was to provide the public with clear descriptions of basic problems and balanced analyses of the fundamental options for dealing with them.

In March, 1985, the Project published "Down . . . Down . . . Down . . . on the Farm," a study of the farm financial crisis written by John C. Obert and William A. Galston. In June, 1985, the Project will publish a monograph by Kenneth Cook concerning resource and environmental issues as they bear on the 1985 farm bill. The current volume, written by William A. Galston, brings together layman's prose with hard numbers to provide an overview of the issues underlying the debate over the 1985 farm bill, the basic options among which our representatives must choose, and the effects of their choice on consumers, farmers, rural Americans, manufacturers, and our trading partners.

In completing this volume we have incurred a number of debts, which it is my pleasure to acknowledge at this time. Foremost is to Economic Perspectives, Incorporated—to J. B. Penn, William Motes, Hosein Shapouri, John Pender, and Susan Wexler—for their invaluable assistance with the early conceptualization of the study, for their detailed empirical analyses of the farm bill options, and for their thorough review of various drafts. We are also indebted to John Obert, Frances Hill, and Robert Lanphier III, who all read the manuscript painstakingly and offered invaluable advice. Special thanks must go to Daniel Gross for research assistance, to Rena Lacey for manuscript production and technical mastery of computer mysteries, and to Jill Leonhardt and Wendy Russell for their unflagging efforts to bring the fruits of our labors before the public. Roger Molander and Michael Higgins, President and Vice President respectively of the Roosevelt Center, provided vital intellectual leadership and moral support throughout.

Special appreciation must go to Richard Dennis, who offered core support for this project as well his continuing personal interest in it, and to the Joyce Foundation, the American Farmland Trust, and the Rockefeller Brothers Fund, all of whom provided funding without which this project could not have been brought to completion.

Susan E. Sechler
April 30, 1985

vii

Introduction

By and large, Americans don't often think about agriculture. Most of us live in or around cities. We take abundant food at reasonable prices for granted. Few of us even know a farmer, let alone engage in farming.

In recent months, however, agriculture has burst onto the national stage. Daily newspapers chronicle the "farm crisis." Nightly television shows farmers demonstrating at state legislatures and blockading commodity exchanges. Movies such as "Country" depict farm families heroically struggling against disaster and foreclosure.

What's happening on the farm? How does it affect citizens who aren't farmers? What can or should we do it about? These are some of the questions this primer on farm policy will try to answer.

These questions are not just urgent; they are unavoidable in 1985. Every four years, the Congress debates and passes the so-called "farm bill." This bill establishes the basic ground-rules for America's farmers and charts a national course for agriculture in areas from nutrition to conservation. Assistance to farmers, agricultural research, food stamps, aid to developing countries—all these programs and many others as well are shaped and funded. This year the farm bill is up for debate once again, and Congressional testimony has already begun.

It would seem natural and proper to use the quadrennial farm bill to reexamine and update the role of government in agriculture. In practice, this has rarely happened. The farm bill is an enormous Christmas tree with roots 50 years deep. Shaping the measure involves horse-trading among dozens of special-interest groups ranging from North Carolina tobacco farmers in the home state of Senate Agriculture Committee Chairman Jesse Helms to urban members of Congress who want to hold the line against cuts in the food stamp program. Having their say along with farm organizations are representatives of big grain companies, officials of multi-billion dollar food processors, and lobbyists for an enormous number of specific commodities. By and large, the debate has been dominated by groups that tend to favor the maintenance or expansion of existing programs. Outsiders with broader concerns or agendas of reform have found it very difficult to make their presence felt in the Congress.

As we head toward consideration of the 1985 farm bill, however, there are signs that "business as usual" may not prevail. Three trends have converged to suggest that the principles and programs governing our approach to agriculture for the past half century may be revised.

In the first place, farm program costs have soared. In 1983, the federal government spent over $28 billion on these programs—more than five times the previous record. Projections for the next four years indicate that if current programs continue unchanged, average annual outlays will far exceed the average for any previous four-year period. At a time when reducing the federal budget deficit is perhaps the most urgent domestic priority, these huge increases have made agricultural programs tempting targets for deep cuts.

Second, these outlays have not created prosperity for rural America. On the contrary: farmers are now facing their worst crisis since the Great Depression. Crushed by a mountain of debt, large numbers may well be driven off their land in the next few years. This prospect has touched off farmer protests and demands for emergency legislation. And it has given rise to serious doubts about the effectiveness of our current approaches.

Third, the basic structure of our agricultural programs has not changed much since their inception during the 1930s. But agriculture itself has been fundamentally transformed. Technological changes and productivity gains have been remarkable. The number of farms and farmers has decreased sharply, while the size of the average farm has almost tripled. Incomes of farm families have risen toward equality with non-farm family incomes. These changes have sparked searching questions about the appropriateness of Depression-era programs for current conditions.

Discussions of farm problems typically fall into two extremes: experts writing in highly technical prose for other experts; and advocates of various causes making their case in highly emotional, even romantic tones. The purpose of this document is different. It seeks to provide legislators and concerned citizens with essential facts about the historical development and current condition of rural America, to set forth and analyze the basic choices for addressing this condition, and to clarify the relation between general goals and specific programs the Congress may well consider in coming months.

Section I

Problems And Perspectives

The purpose of Section I is to introduce some central concerns of contemporary American agriculture and some important ways of thinking about them.

Chapter 1 discusses the changing role of agriculture in our country and provides a capsule history of the relation between public policy and agricultural development.

Chapter 2 examines some of the fundamental issues that will guide us in choosing responses to current problems: key changes in agriculture and rural America since the inception of New Deal farm programs; debate about appropriate goals for future agricultural policy; and ways in which differing conceptions of appropriate means can serve to structure and constrain public policy.

Chapter 1

The Place of Farming
In Our National Life

Culture and Politics

The discussion of agricultural policy properly begins with a glance at the unique place agriculture—especially the "family farm"—occupies in our national culture.

The United States began as an agricultural nation. At the time the Constitution was adopted, over 90 percent of the population lived and worked on farms. Farming made up virtually all of our gross national product.

Agriculture was of more than economic significance. Political leaders such as Thomas Jefferson feared what they saw as the corruption of city life, with its extremes of wealth and poverty, and power and dependence. Cities, they felt, tended to produce a combustible combination of oligarchs and rabble. "The mobs of great cities," wrote Jefferson, "add just so much to the support of pure government, as sores do to the strength of the human body." Rural life, by contrast, was thought to engender true citizens— independent individuals whose lives were guided by reason and common sense, who cherished hard work, respected the dignity and equality of others, and embodied all the democratic virtues. Jefferson memorably summarized this agrarian faith: "Those who labor in the earth are the chosen people of God, if ever he had a chosen people, whose breasts he has made his peculiar deposit for substantial and genuine virtue." Such citizens, he argued, could be counted on to make prudent political decisions, to take care of most problems at the local level, and to guard against dangerous concentrations of potentially tyrannical power.

As the American economy expanded and diversified, farmers made up a steadily shrinking fraction of our population and workforce. But the agricultural way of life retained its cultural centrality. Indeed, as industrialization swept the country in the generation after the Civil War, the defenders of rural America used farming as a symbolic antidote to all the ills of the modern life. City life was artificial; rural life was close to nature. City life

3

was rootless and lonely; rural life affirmed the value of community, family, and caring among the generations. City life was driven by unlimited greed; rural life asked for only a modest and decent livelihood. Farmers produced real wealth, while capitalists of every stripe—railroad barons, financiers, commodity speculators—shuffled paper assets and engaged in legalized theft . . . mainly from farmers. In the silent movies made around the turn of the century, the most common motif was the "city slicker" who was out to bamboozle, cheat, or foreclose on the poor, innocent, but virtuous farm family. But however powerless and oppressed, farmers remained the mainstay of our society. The populist Democrat William Jennings Bryan proclaimed that

> Burn down your cities and leave our farms, and your cities will spring up again as if by magic; but destroy our farms, and the grass will grow in the streets of every city in the country.

Even today, the image of rural life has not wholly lost its resonance. "Getting back to nature" remains a classic American urge, whether in the rural communes of the 1960s or the more solitary farms of contemporary achievers fed up with the urban rat race. Within the past year, widely-viewed films such as "Places in the Heart" and "Country" have evoked different aspects of this romance of the rural. Not surprisingly, politicians and rural advocates depict dire social consequences of the collapse of the "family farm" to rally public support for a wide range of government intervention.

Early History

The contemporary debate over farm policy is, in a sense, nothing new. For most of our history, the development and health of agriculture have been matters of public concern. But the nature of public involvement has shifted over time in response to changes in both national needs and the situation of America's farmers.

The first important phase of public activity began in the mid-1800s. Its goals were to settle vacant lands and expand agricultural production. To achieve these goals, government provided incentives for new settlers, subsidized agricultural research and education, and helped farmers to get the supplies, credit, and information they needed to produce efficiently. For example, the Homestead Act of 1862 made small land parcels available to prospective farmers at little or no cost, and federal encouragement for the transcontinental railroad opened vast reaches of the country to settlers and new markets.

Many of the agricultural institutions we still take for granted today were put in place during this period. The Department of Agriculture was created in 1862, with the initial purpose of dispensing improved seeds and technical

4

information to farmers. In that same year, Congress enacted the Morrill Act, which made federal lands available to the states to found agricultural colleges (the "land grant" colleges). In 1887, passage of the Hatch Act led to the system of state agricultural experiment stations, intended to develop advanced technology for farmers.

Beyond information, Congress offered farmers a range of material assistance. The Land Reclamation Act of 1902 provided subsidized irrigation water from federal projects. The Federal Farm Loan Act of 1916 created the 12 cooperative Federal Land Banks and the beginnings of today's Farm Credit System, the single largest agricultural lender.

This burst of creative legislation had a number of important results. The settlement of land had proceeded rapidly, and the number of farms had grown to more than six million. Agricultural production rose steadily if undramatically. Farmers enjoyed higher incomes and purchasing power, and the quality of rural life improved markedly. It is not hard to understand why farmers regard the first two decades of the twentieth century as the Golden Age of American agriculture and use the status they enjoyed during that period as the benchmark for judging their subsequent condition.

While farmers were satisfied with their lot, the country as a whole was not satisfied with the performance of the agricultural sector. During the early part of the twentieth century, agricultural productivity stagnated, and overall production rose far less than did our population. The result was a squeeze on supplies and rapidly escalating consumer prices, especially for city dwellers. These developments produced a wave of urban criticism of allegedly stodgy, out of date, and selfish farmers. And it led to government efforts to improve agricultural productivity and reduce commodity prices. The Smith-Lever Act of 1914 created the cooperative federal-state Agricultural Extension Service to disseminate information and new technology to farmers. The Smith-Hughes Act of 1917 provided federal support for agricultural instruction in public high schools.

These moves were at first resisted by farmers, many of whom sensed the emphasis on productivity as a threat. But eventually changes in agricultural production began to take hold and, along with the conclusion of the boom sparked by World War One, helped bring the Golden Age to an end. The wartime surge in demand subsided, and agricultural production in Europe returned to more normal levels. Farm prices collapsed. Wheat went from $2.16 a bushel in 1919 to just $1.03 in 1920. Farm income declined by nearly one-half. Throughout the 1920s, as the rest of the economy roared ahead, farm incomes continued to decline. Discontented farmers sought to restore past prosperity and preserve their way of life from further changes. They began calling for "100 percent of parity": If a bushel of wheat had bought, say, a new shirt between 1910 and 1914, then it should do so in the 1920s—indeed, forever. And if the market did not yield this result, then

5

the government should step in to guarantee it. Bills to this effect were twice passed by the Congress, and twice vetoed by President Coolidge.

Then the bottom fell out. With the onset of the Great Depression in 1929, declining purchasing power reduced demand for agricultural products at home and abroad. Rising trade barriers only made matters worse. Between 1929 and 1932, prices fell an additional 56 percent, while net farm income fell 70 percent. At the low point of the Great Depression, the income of the average farm family was only two-fifths that of the average non-farm family. Rural distress spilled over into violence as mobs of farmers forcibly resisted foreclosures and demanded relief from hardpressed banks and state treasuries.

The farmers' problems went far deeper than declining income. The modernization sweeping most of America had passed rural America by. Farm families lacked electricity and telephones. Rural roads were dirt. Sewers and water mains were nonexistent. Basic services such as education and health care were far below national standards.

As if this were not bad enough, farmers were vulnerable—in some cases increasingly vulnerable—to natural disasters. The lack of effective flood control exposed farmers to periodic extremes of water shortages and inundation. Inappropriate cropping practices together with inadequate soil conservation and sustained drought yielded the devastation of the Dust Bowl.

To improve their lot, farmers had only one effective resource—the power of numbers. Farm families comprised one-fourth of the total population. All rural Americans together made up nearly one-half the population. Over one half of the 435 Congressional districts were classified as farm districts, with a farm population of at least 20 percent. During the mid-1930s, the political will born of rural desperation joined hands with the reform spirit of the New Deal to produce the second great phase of creative farm policy.

The New Deal

In agriculture, as in most areas, the New Deal proceeded through trial and error. Nevertheless, it is possible to discern four basic assumptions that helped structure New Deal activities in this area.

First, it was generally acknowledged that the ''free market'' had failed. Accordingly, the case for public action was greatly strengthened.

Second, the economies of the industrialized nations had turned inward during the Depression, and the importance of trade had diminished. The American economy could therefore be treated as a closed system, and efforts to help the farmer could focus almost exclusively on the domestic market.

6

Third, the moral entitlement of farmers was felt to be beyond serious question. They were vital to our economy and society, but they were sinking through no fault of their own.

Finally, they were all in more or less the same boat; differences among farmers were dwarfed by the commonality of their plight. Programs could therefore be directed toward alleviating the misery and elevating the status of all farmers—indeed, of all rural Americans.

The New Deal sought to address four key rural problems: inadequate income, poor quality of life, injustice, and vulnerability to natural disaster.

1. Income

To increase farm income, the federal government pursued four basic strategies. The first was, in effect, to guarantee farmers certain minimum prices for their products through the Commodity Credit Corporation (CCC), established in 1933. The program worked like this:

- By pledging a quantity of certain commodities as collateral, farmers could obtain loans from the CCC at market or below-market rates of interest. These loans were made at a fixed price (known as the "loan rate") per unit of each commodity.
- Within the period specified by the loan, the borrower had a choice: to regain control of the commodity pledged as collateral by repaying the loan, or to default. In the latter case, the CCC then owned the commodity, and the borrower was considered to have discharged his loan obligation, including the accumulated interest.

This program guaranteed that farmers would get no less than the loan rate for each unit of production. And it ensured the availability of short-term loans that allowed farmers to store their crops in the hope of higher prices later in the marketing season.

Inherent in this strategy was a problem that had already become apparent with previous loan/storage programs during the Hoover administration. If the supply of commodities exceeded demand, not just occasionally, but chronically, then the government would accumulate huge surpluses and incur large loan and storage costs. Farmers would have no incentive to help stabilize market prices by cutting production to bring supply back in line with demand. On the contrary: they would be rewarded for continuing to overproduce.

Accordingly, the CCC loan program was buttressed by a second New Deal farm income strategy: direct government efforts to reduce production. Various tactics were employed, such as limits on the amount of specific commodities each farmer could sell on the market and restrictions on the number of acres each farmer could plant. Behind these tactics stood one basic premise: relatively small cuts in production would significantly raise market prices, more than compensating the farmer for a lower volume of sales.

These production controls, the heart of the Agricultural Adjustment Act of 1933, represented a fundamental change from what had been near-total reliance on market forces to extensive federal intervention in individual decisions. Upon signing this bill into law, President Roosevelt commented:

> I tell you frankly that it is a new and untrod path, but I can tell you with equal frankness that an unprecedented condition calls for the trial of new means.

In a third effort to bolster farm income, the New Deal sought, not just to regulate supply, but also to boost demand. School lunch programs, direct commodity distribution, and other nutritional programs were put in place during this period, and the food stamp program was conceived. These efforts combined concern for alleviating misery throughout our society with a narrower focus on helping farmers dispose of what would otherwise have been surplus production.

Finally, the New Deal recognized that many farmers needed affordable credit to avoid bankruptcy, modernize their operations, and achieve economic self-sufficiency. Legislation passed during this period provided loans to hardpressed farmers and financed a wide range of capital improvements.

2. Quality of Life

The second great goal of New Deal agricultural legislation was to improve the quality of rural life. To this end, landmark policies were put in place. The Rural Electrification plan brought electricity and telephone service to all but the most remote farms. Rural Free Delivery provided prompt and regular mail service. Road and bridge construction helped reduce rural isolation. (This trend was to be spurred in the 1950s by the decision to create the interstate highway system.) Government information and aid helped consolidate one-room rural schoolhouses into modern elementary and secondary schools. Similarly, the gap between rural and urban health care began to close. The New Deal, in short, set in motion a process that brought rural Americans into the mainstream of American life.

3. Justice

The third great goal of New Deal agricultural legislation was to ameliorate rural injustice. During the late 1920s and early 1930s, scholars and activists began to document the twin rural evils of poverty and powerlessness, which were traced to the practice of tenant farming, or sharecropping. It was argued that unless farmers were aided to purchase their own land, they would be at the mercy of landowners, who would inevitably take advantage of their power to set terms that would guarantee permanent subordination and servitude.

To address these problems, President Roosevelt issued an Executive Order early in 1935 creating the Resettlement Administration. After two years of controversy over the goals and policies of this agency, Congress passed the Bankhead-Jones Farm Tenant Act, which transfered the powers of the Resettlement Administration to USDA (under the name of the "Farm Security Administration") and authorized federal loans for land purchase to qualified tenant farmers, as well as a range of other programs to assist former tenants in making the transition to independent operations and prevent debt-ridden small farmers from defaulting on their loans and slipping back into tenant status. Although these efforts were subject to constant attack from entrenched interests (particularly in the South), tens of thousands of tenant farmers were nevertheless enabled to escape their former powerlessness and become self-sufficient owners of their own small plots of land.

4. Protection Against Disaster

The fourth great goal of New Deal agricultural legislation was to protect farmers against natural disasters—including some to which their own shortsightedness had contributed. To improve practices that had exhausted the soil and fostered erosion in the Dust Bowl and elsewhere, the Soil Conservation Service was made a permanent part of the Department of Agriculture. Working through locally elected boards, it gained responsibility for soil and water conservation policies throughout the United States. To reduce the severity and impact of floods, the federal government financed thousands of dams and water projects. And to help out farmers who suffered devastation from bad weather or other "acts of God", the Federal Crop Insurance Program was established in 1938, and supplemented in 1949 with the Disaster Loan Act that provided emergency loans to stricken farmers.

Post-New Deal Developments

The New Deal programs did help relieve the worst misery and stabilize the agricultural sector. They did not, however, bring supply and demand into balance. That occurred only under the influence of World War II and postwar food shortages in Europe and Asia. And it was temporary. Starting in the late 1940s, productivity increases accelerated as agriculture became much more mechanized and new hybrid seeds and breeds were introduced.

This surge in productivity had two main effects. First, Americans left their farms for the cities in record numbers. As late as 1940, more than 30 million lived and worked on farms. By 1960, that figure had been cut in half. Second, massive surpluses returned, and government storage facilities sprang up throughout the country to hold the growing commodity stocks.

The federal government responded in two ways. First, it resumed and expanded production controls. The Soil Bank Program, enacted in 1956, paid farmers to idle land. Between 1961 and 1972, an average of 12 percent of all cropland was idled. Second, the government sought to expand exports through foreign food aid programs and export subsidies. These efforts, along with postwar world economic recovery and population growth, led to steady if unspectacular growth in exports during the 1950s and 1960s.

In the 1970s, many factors converged to produce a full-fledged agricultural export boom. Expanding economies and rising personal incomes boosted demand throughout the developing world. The Soviet Union, once a net exporter, abruptly became one of the largest grain importers. Resumption of diplomatic and trade relations with the People's Republic of China reopened a market that had been closed for almost two generations. OPEC's sudden new wealth increased the appetite of oil-producing nations for agricultural imports.

General economic conditions and agricultural policies also contributed to rising exports. Credit was plentiful, and real interest rates were low. Devaluations of the dollar in the early 1970s made American products much more affordable on world markets.

The massive Soviet grain purchases starting in 1972 were the spark igniting the export explosion, which continued until 1981. During this period, export volume grew 9.4 percent annually, double the rate of the preceding twenty years. Correcting for inflation, the value of these exports rose by nearly 150 percent. By 1980, exports provided 29 percent of cash received by farmers, and nearly two-fifths of the cropland was producing for export.

Table 1.
Export Boom

Item	1973	1974	1975	1976	1977	1978	1979	1980
	— — — billion dollars — — —							
Total	17.6	21.9	21.9	22.7	24.0	27.3	32.0	40.5
Developed Countries	9.7	11.3	11.1	13.1	14.9	15.2	17.4	21.1
Developing Countries	6.7	10.1	9.5	6.9	7.4	8.9	10.2	13.7
Centrally Planned Countries	1.2	0.5	1.3	2.7	1.7	3.2	4.4	5.7

The export boom brought many changes to U. S. agriculture. The most immediate result was unprecedented prosperity. Prices rose rapidly. Net farm income set new records. The per capita income of farmers surpassed nonfarm incomes for the first time ever. Farm asset values (primarily land), corrected for inflation, rose by nearly half. Farm debt quadrupled as farmers borrowed against their increased land values to finance expansion and modernization. (As a percentage of total production expenses, interest payments on debt roughly doubled during that period.)

The benefits of this new prosperity extended throughout rural America. Providers of farm supplies, equipment, and services prospered as production expanded rapidly. New employment opportunities opened up in rural communities. Businesses that processed and exported agricultural products posted record profits.

The country as a whole benefitted in several ways. The agricultural trade surplus helped counterbalance the declining competitiveness of American manufactured goods in world markets. Government expenditures to support farmers, store surpluses, and idle cropland declined sharply as government policy shifted toward encouraging rather than limiting production.

While the benefits of the export surge were pronounced, some problems emerged as well. Increased demand significantly raised food prices and contributed to the inflationary surge of the 1970s. The poorer developing countries without oil revenues were doubly disadvantaged as the cost of imported food rose while U. S. food aid declined by two-thirds. And the environmental consequences of high production attracted increased concern. Soil erosion accelerated as large areas of fragile land were cultivated. Irrigation expanded, imperiling long-term water supplies. The widespread use of chemical fertilizers and pesticides raised fears about human health and the ecological balance.

At just the moment when U. S. agricultural policy came to rest on the premise of ever-expanding exports, the boom was halted and reversed in the early 1980s. As inflation came to be perceived as intolerable, the Federal Reserve Board shifted to a tight-money policy, which reduced the pace of economic activity at home and abroad. The global recession reduced demand. Exacerbated by unprecedented U.S. budget deficits, high real interest rates impeded imports among developing nations that relied on credit. OPEC nations slowed their imports in response to declining oil revenues. Overall, the value of world agricultural trade declined by 10 percent between 1980 and 1982.

American exports were even harder hit. The rapid rise in the value of the dollar reduced the competitiveness of U. S. products while making it easier for foreign producers to penetrate traditional U.S. markets. The European Economic Community increased its access to world markets by heavily subsidizing agricultural exports. The 1980 grain embargo against the Soviet Union further damaged U.S. exports by tarnishing the U. S. reputation as a reliable supplier, helping nations such as Argentina to compete with us. Government policy overreacted by paying farmers to idle a record number of acres in 1983. When drought unexpectedly struck during the summer of that year, very high U.S. feed grain prices helped foreign exporters further increase their share of the world market. As a result of all this, the volume

11

of American agricultural exports declined by 11 percent between 1981 and 1983, while their value fell by a full 20 percent. (Exports recovered somewhat in 1984, but the outlook for 1985 is dismal.)

Table 2.
Export Bust

Item	: 1981	1982	1983	1984	1985 (Estimate)
	— — — billion dollars — — —				
Total	43.8	39.1	34.8	38.0	34.1
Developed Countries	21.9	20.5	18.5	19.2	
Developing Countries	16.3	13.5	13.9	14.9	
Centrally Planned Countries	5.6	5.1	2.4	3.9	

This decline in exports precipitated a steep recession in the agricultural economy. Net farm income was cut in half between 1981 and 1983 before recovering modestly in 1984. Land values declined for four consecutive years—the sharpest decline since the Depression. Caught between falling land values, plunging crop prices, and rising real interest rates, many farmers found it difficult to pay off loans taken out during the boom. In the past year, farm credit has moved from a problem to a full-fledged crisis. Many mid-sized commercial farmers—some experts believe one-quarter of the total, or even more—may be driven off their land in the next few years if nothing is done. (For a fuller discussion of this issue, see Chapter 5.)

The agricultural recession has extended well beyond farmers. Rural banks have been hard pressed, and many have closed. The sale of farm equipment has plunged over 50 percent; dealerships have closed at record rates; manufacturers have laid off over 140,000 workers; and giant corporations such as International Harvester have teetered on the brink of bankruptcy. Fertilizer and pesticide sales have declined. Agricultural processors and exporters are suffering.

Taxpayers have been hard-hit as well. The cost of farm programs rose tremendously, from an average of $3 billion annually in the 1970s to $12 billion in 1982 and more than $28 billion in 1983 before dropping back in 1984 as the PIK program ended.

As we head into the debate over the 1985 farm bill, there is a growing sense of desperation among rural Americans, urgency among public officials, and confusion among citizens and taxpayers. There is widespread public sympathy for embattled farmers and a general sense that something should be done. But there the agreement ends, as advocates of the free market inside and outside the administration clash with proponents of vigorous government intervention. Thinking through some of the fundamental questions raised by this debate is the purpose of the next chapter.

SELECTED REFERENCES

Sidney Baldwin, *Poverty and Politics: The Rise and Decline of the Farm Security Administration*. The University of North Carolina Press, 1968.

David B. Danbom, *The Resisted Revolution: Urban America and the Industrialization of Agriculture, 1900-1930*. The Iowa State University Press, 1979.

Don Paarlberg, "Effects of New Deal Farm Programs on the Agricultural Agenda A Half Century Later and Prospect for the Future." American Agricultural Economics Association Annual Meeting, August 1983.

B. R. Robinson, "Fifty Years of Farm Policy: What Have We Learned?" American Association for the Advancement of Science Annual Meeting, May 1984.

Wayne D. Rasmussen, "The Historic Role of the Federal Government in Agricultural Policy." Economic Research Service, USDA, February 1985.

Chapter 2

Thinking About Agricultural Policy

Fashioning a sound approach to the problems of modern agriculture is more than a technical exercise of comparing numbers and programs. It demands as well a reexamination of the basic premises that shape our understanding of both agriculture and public policy.

There are three key questions that will help guide our inquiry.

First, in what ways have agriculture and rural America changed since the programs of the New Deal were enacted, and what are the implications of these changes for public policy?

Second, in what ways (if any) have our goals changed since the New Deal, and how does this affect future policy?

Third, what kinds of means are we willing to employ in pursuit of the goals we select, and how do they structure (or constrain) policy choices?

Changes

In 1920, the farm population was 32 million—30 percent of our total population. Thirty years later, in 1950, only 15 percent of the population lived on farms. And each decade since then, that percentage has been cut roughly in half again. Today, the farm population is only 2.4 percent of the total—about 5.6 million people.

This doesn't mean that agricultural production has declined. On the contrary: production today is roughly two and one-half times what it was in 1920. The reason is higher productivity. Each acre of land yields more than twice as much as it did 60 years ago. Each agricultural worker produces more than ten times as much. Improved seeds, fertilizers, pesticides, and equipment are some of the factors that have spurred this astonishing growth.

Another factor is the steady increase in farm size. The amount of land under cultivation hasn't changed much since 1920, but it is managed quite differently. Then there were more than 6 million farms, averaging well under 200 acres each. Today there are about 2.25 million farms averaging 437 acres. (Of this total, only about one-quarter—the 670,000 with annual sales of $40,000 or more—should be considered commercial farms.) On balance, these larger farms have been more able to afford and to use the technological improvements that have spurred productivity. In fact, since 1920 there has been a kind of circular relation. The rapid increase in productivity that follows new technology tends to increase the scale of concentration of production. In turn, the high returns realized by innovators enlarge the market for new technology. The worth of the average farm has also increased—in fact, far more rapidly than its size. Average net worth (assets minus debts, corrected for inflation) is eight times what it was 60 years ago.

Through the 1970s, farm incomes also rose dramatically, both in absolute terms and relative to the rest of the population. At the depth of the Great Depression, per capita farm income was only 39 percent of nonfarm income. By the 1970s, that figure had soared to 87 percent. Even in this decade, a comparatively depressed period for agriculture, it is nearly 80 percent. If we look at family (as opposed to individual) incomes, the picture is even brighter. In 1983, average income for farm families slightly exceeded that of nonfarm families.

Changes concealed by these averages are just as striking. At the onset of the New Deal, most farms were pretty much alike. Today, the differences are enormous. Three-quarters have annual sales under $40,000, accounting together for only 13 percent of total output. At the other extreme, large operations with sales of $500,000 and over account for only 1 percent of farms but nearly 30 percent of total output.

Sources of farm income have shifted considerably. In our grandparents' time, most of the income received by farm families came from farming. Today, on average, farm families earn $1.47 from outside sources for every $1.00 from farming. For most small and mid-size farmers, outside earnings come from service or manufacturing jobs in nearby communities.

The composition of family income varies sharply with farm size. Families living on very small farms with sales under $40,000 derive nearly all their income from off-farm employment. (In fact, most of them lose money on farming and subsidize their losses from the outside.) As farm size rises, so too does the percentage of total income from farming.

Farm debt describes a similar pattern. The smallest farms have the lowest ratio of debt to assets. The larger the farm, the larger (on average) is the percentage of indebtedness.

These two facts—source of income and relative debt levels—suggest that the vulnerability of farms to economic fluctuations also varies by size. The smallest farms are less affected by changes in commodity prices and interest rates. The very largest farms tend to earn relatively high profits on invested capital and to have very substantial assets on which they can draw to tide them over one or two rough years. Hardest hit are the moderate-size farms, highly dependent on favorable commodity prices, heavily in debt, and with-

16

out adequate reserves of cash or reasonably liquid assets. For the most part, the operators of these mid-size farms are the ones you see on television demanding action from Congress and state legislatures.

Rising incomes and assets have revolutionized farming over the past half century. But even broader changes have spread throughout rural America, altering rural life not just quantitatively, but qualitatively, in two key respects.

First, the countryside is vastly different. Programs put in place during the New Deal have helped bring most rural Americans into the mainstream of American life. Electricity, telephones, indoor plumbing, modern roads and transportation, education, and health care—all these and more, rare in the 1930s, are virtually universal today throughout rural America. Farming is still hard, demanding work. But it is not now, as it was 50 years ago, so cut off from the rest of society. As a social class, farmers and rural Americans are much more like the rest of us than they were two generations ago.

Second, the economic isolation of agriculture has been greatly reduced. In our grandparents' time, the individual farm was largely self-contained. It created most of its own supplies. It was dependent on labor, especially work performed by family members, rather than capital or machinery. It produced a wide range of commodities, which could provide farm families subsistence even in hard times.

Today, by contrast, farmers purchase nearly 60 percent of everything they use. Farm labor has declined sharply, replaced by sophisticated and costly machinery. (The average farm worker is now backed up by twice as much investment in equipment as is the average worker in our economy.) Typically, an individual farm specializes in a narrow range of commodities and uses the income generated from their sale to buy goods and services produced by others. For these reasons, it has been argued that today's farmer should be viewed, not as a worker, but as the owner of a small manufacturing operation, purchasing raw materials from the outside, processing them, and then selling them in external markets.

In short, the independence of the family farm is all but gone, replaced by a complex two-way relation to the local and national economy. Although the direct sale of farm products accounts for only 2 percent of gross national product (GNP), the overall food and agriculture system (equipment and supplies, transportation, processing, and marketing) accounts for more than one-fifth of GNP and total employment. When agricultural production and income fall, therefore, the effects ripple through rural America (where 60 million people still live) and through the broader economy. Conversely, inflation, high interest rates, and other national economic ills have a significant, sometimes overwhelming, effect on the conduct of agriculture. (For a fuller discussion of this relationship, see Chapter 3.)

17

This new exposure (and vulnerability) of agriculture extends far beyond our borders. In 1920, agricultural exports were only about $2 billion. As late as 1970, they totalled only $7 billion. And then came an unprecedented export surge, which peaked in 1981 at more than $43 billion. Even today, after three years of world recession in agricultural trade, it exceeds $34 billion, and the surplus (exports minus imports) offsets about $20 billion of our soaring deficit in manufactured goods.

The farm economy depends heavily on exports. Of every ten acres devoted to agriculture in this country, nearly four are producing for foreign markets. Of every dollar of agricultural sales, 30 cents comes from exports. If the ratio of foreign sales to total production were to slip back to 1970 levels, more than one in ten farmers would be forced out of business. Exports lost during the past three years have already depressed commodity prices and farm incomes. And because our ability to produce agricultural goods increases more rapidly than our ability to consume them, the failure to increase exports steadily in the future will ensure a continuing squeeze on farmers.

Of the many inferences that can be drawn from these changes, the following are the most significant for our understanding of agricultural policy.

1. Three of the key goals of New Deal farm policy—reducing the gap between farm and nonfarm incomes, attacking rural servitude and oppression, and bringing rural Americans into the mainstream of our national life—have been substantially advanced.

2. The fourth New Deal goal—protecting farmers against disaster—has been only partly fulfilled. Dams, water projects, and insurance schemes have ameliorated the effects of flood, drought, and bad weather. On the other hand, problems such as soil erosion and exhaustion, and water depletion and pollution, have actually intensified.

3. Because farms are now far more diverse in size and source of income than they were 50 years ago, universal programs open to all farmers make far less sense, while the need for sensible targeting has increased.

4. Because farms now form the base of a complex food system, farm programs can have effects far beyond their direct beneficiaries. Raising the price of one commodity may have an adverse effect on producers of other commodities. Drastically reducing production may devastate producers of farm equipment and supplies. As we evaluate future farm programs, their broader economic consequences must be explicitly taken into account.

5. Because farming is now integrated into the national economy, it is far more affected by changes in economic policy. High interest rates severely affect farmers, who are far more dependent on credit than are most other sectors. An overvalued dollar hits them again by reducing the attractiveness of their products overseas while giving new opportunities to our foreign competitors. To the extent that these ills can be traced to unprecedented

budget deficits, the agricultural sector has an enormous stake in the outcome of the current deficit reduction debate.

6.   Because American agriculture is now integrated into the international economy, programs that treat the American market as a closed system are outdated. Prices are affected by world supplies, not just domestic supplies. Farm incomes are affected by export competitiveness, not just domestic sales. Demand for our agricultural products is influenced by our reputation as a reliable (or unreliable) supplier. Agricultural prosperity is affected by the subsidies and trade barriers of other nations, which are influenced in turn by American economic policy and diplomacy. For these reasons, assumptions about the future role of American agriculture in the world economy now critically influence the way we think about future agricultural policies.

Goals

These basic changes over the past half-century provide the context within which food and agriculture programs must be reevaluated. But the choices we make will reflect, not only these facts, but also the goals we adopt for food and agriculture policies.

There is less than full agreement on appropriate goals. Some proposals are more controversial, others less so. Not infrequently, apparent consensus dissolves as various participants in the debate offer differing interpretations of key terms. And in agriculture, as in every other area, cherished goals can come into conflict. Individuals who agree with one another on a list of goals can nevertheless disagree about how conflicts among them are to be resolved.

The following discussion will attempt to survey and evaluate the key proposed goals for modern food and agriculture policies, looking at areas both of consensus and of controversy.

1.   Food Quality, Quantity, Availability, and Price

Most Americans would agree to the following general goal for food and agriculture policy: Our food supply should be abundant, nutritious, safe, and reasonably priced, and an adequate diet should be available to everyone. Indeed, in many respects we have come to take the achievement of this goal for granted.

It is easy to forget just how fortunate we are in this regard. Our rich resources of soil and water, coupled with successful public and private investments in increased productivity, have made our agricultural system the envy of the world. We recognize our favored status only intermittently, when we read about massive food shortfalls in the Soviet Union or watch televised reports about widespread famine in Africa.

19

Yet even within this rather complacent consensus, important disagreements can surface. Consider, for example, the issue of food safety.

For most of human history, food production and preparation were the province of the household and local community. People knew where and how their food was grown and processed. But in the latter part of the 19th century, improved storage and transportation brought increased long-distance trade in food products. Consumers became less sure of food quality and less able to verify claims made by manufacturers, who engaged in frequent adulteration of foodstuffs and used a range of unsavory processing techniques. Muckraking reports raised public consciousness of these abuses and led to widespread legislation and regulation of foods and additives on both the federal and state levels.

As food growth and processing became more complex, the concept of safety became increasingly elusive. In 1958, for example, federal law required premarket testing of all new additives, prohibited the use of new additives not shown to be safe, and stipulated that "no additive shall be deemed to be safe if it is found to induce cancer when ingested by man or animal." This stipulation (known as the "Delaney clause") has become a focal point for intense debate among both scientists and policy-makers. Some argue that the fact that massive amounts of a substance will induce cancer should not lead to a total ban if it would be present in our food supply in far lower quantities per serving. This argument leads to the conclusion that we should set specific quantitative limits on the use of such substances while informing the public of possible risks. Others argue that we do not know enough about cancer-causing agents to set such standards and that given the objective of safeguarding health and life, the most stringent approach is the only appropriate one.

If safety were the only goal of food policy, this argument would be decisive. But as we have already seen, it is not. Many controversial substances (pesticides, growth hormones, preservatives, and the like) favorably affect food quantity, quality, availability, and price. Farmers and food processors argue that when they are forbidden to use these substances, consumers ultimately suffer. Such arguments raise difficult issues. How much risk (if any) is tolerable? What kinds of compromises (if any) are permissible between health and safety, on the one hand, and other desirable features of our food production and distribution system?

Other portions of this first goal are equally controversial. Consider "abundance." One interpretation of this would be that our food production should be measured by our domestic needs and that exports should be treated as a residual—that is, whatever happens to be left over after domestic demand has been satisfied. Another interpretation is that worldwide market demand must somehow be accommodated. A third is that our production must be large enough to alleviate world hunger, especially for those nations that cannot afford to buy everything they need in the free market. And abundance is sensitive to time-horizon and instability. In the face of natural disasters, surpluses can quickly turn into shortages. How much of our production in good times should be placed in reserve for the bad times? Whose responsibility is it to make and act upon this determination—the federal government, farmers, consumers?

Abundance can also conflict with other things we want. If commodities cannot be transported across long distances, they cannot be made available to consumers in geographically dispersed markets. To make this possible, certain products may have to be specially bred for their resistance to damage during shipment, and this can have negative affects on flavor and nutrition. (Tomatoes are a familiar example of this problem.) Increased processing has also contributed to abundance, at some cost to nutrition. And efforts to ensure abundance can have pronounced effects on prices. In 1973, for example, an embargo on soybean exports designed to preserve adequate domestic supplies helped cause a 50 percent drop in prices, which farmers understandably regarded as unreasonable and unfair.

The question of price is of course inherently controversial. American consumers tend to be relatively satisfied about food prices—and with good reason. On average, they spend less than one out of every six dollars of disposable income on food, and the percentage continues to decline. Today it is the lowest in the world. (By contrast, consumers in many other industrialized nations must use well over 20 percent of their income for food, while Soviet citizens spend over 30 percent.)

Farmers are far less satisfied. Federal farm programs in part arose in response to complaints from farmers that they were not receiving fair prices for their products. But defining fairness has proved to be no easy matter.

Some farmers and farm organizations argue that commodity prices should reach "parity"—that is, the level equal to the purchasing power units of commodities enjoyed in the golden years of American agriculture (1910-1914). But broad acceptance of this parity standard has declined in recent decades. Among other difficulties, it wholly disregards the staggering changes in agricultural productivity during this century. (Imagine the response if the makers of transistors or computers demanded the same relative price for each unit of their product as they received 20 years ago.)

Another frequently invoked standard of fair price is "cost of production." Intuitively, the proposition that farmers ought to be able to sell their products for at least what it cost to make them seems sensible. But this standard, too, turns out to have severe limitations. Costs are not uniform. Some farmers have much higher costs than others. If prices are set to meet the higher costs (as is done by the European Common Market) then massive overproduction is inevitable. If prices correspond to the costs of the most efficient producers, then the demands of all the others (who tend to be the

21

ones complaining) will not be satisfied.

A third possible standard is total income. As we have seen, this measure yields mixed results. Per capita farm income is below per capita nonfarm income, but family income is roughly equal between the two sectors. Size and composition of income varies sharply with farm size.

The least misleading measure may be what economists call "total return"—income from farm operations plus capital gains from land and other assets. The figures are revealing. From 1940 to 1983, average annual total return from farming has been roughly equal to the figure for other investments such as common stocks. Within this period, variations are considerable. During the 1970s, the return from farming far exceeded that obtained from stocks. In the 1980s, the reverse has been true. This suggests that the current distress (which is real) should not be allowed to obscure the very substantial farm/nonfarm equilibrium that has existed over time. At the same time, the experience of the 1970s indicates that if too much of total return is derived from capital gains and too little from operations, the overall situation of farmers is dangerously unstable. Inflation-induced increases in land values are no substitute in the long run for solid yearly incomes from farming.

It is easy to imagine that the interests of farmers and consumers on matters of price are directly opposed, that if consumers are satisfied farmers will be hurting, or the reverse. In fact, the relationship between what farmers get and what consumers pay has become much less direct over time. Today, on average, only 26 cents of each food dollar goes to the farmer. The other 74 cents goes to those who transport, process, and sell it to consumers in finished form. Thus, a 10 percent increase in farm commodity prices would raise food prices by only 2.6 percent, and the general level of inflation by only 0.5 percent.

Although current prices are relatively tolerable for average Americans, that is not the case for the poor, some of whom must spend 50 percent of their disposable incomes on food. Hunger and malnutrition are far from unknown in America, although their extent is a matter of intense political dispute today.

Programs to deal with these problems began during the New Deal, gradually expanded during the postwar period, and grew explosively during the 1960s and 1970s. Today, more than 20 million people receive food stamps. 23 million children eat subsidized school lunches. Millions more pregnant women and infants participate in a range of nutrition programs. As these numbers have risen, so have the costs. Total expenditures for food assistance rose from $1 billion in 1969 to $19 billion in 1984.

Few Americans would disagree with the underlying proposition that society has a responsibility to ensure that an adequate diet is available to all. But putting such a diet within everyone's reach does not in any way guar-

22

antee that everyone will have a balanced, nutritious diet. Some argue that choice of food is wholly the responsibility of each individual. Others argue that the government has a responsibility to spread information about sound nutrition and actively educate consumers—especially the poor and disadvantaged, who are usually the least able to make wise use of available resources. This was actually tried during the late 1970s. Understandably, cattle, dairy, and egg producers did not react enthusiastically to calls for reducing fat and cholesterol consumption. Here once again was a clash between key elements of an apparently consensual goal—in this case, nutrition on the one hand versus demand, and therefore price, on the other.

2. Conservation

Most Americans would assent to a second general goal: Agricultural policy should help preserve the land and water needed for future agricultural production, and it should help safeguard our environment for future generations.

Widespread support for this goal is of relatively recent origin. For most of our country's history, we took abundant natural resources for granted. Our principal objective was to develop and exploit them.

The emphasis first began to shift in the late 1920s, when careful studies revealed that soil erosion was more threatening than had previously been believed. But it was the spectacle of disastrous droughts and dust storms throughout the plains states in 1935 and 1936 (the so-called "Dust Bowl") that galvanized the nation. The New Deal responded with agencies and programs designed to instruct and assist farmers in sound longterm soil conservation practices. Major efforts included idling erosive land, substituting nonerosive for erosive crops, and improving management of water supplies. Once the Dust Bowl crisis had subsided, however, attention to resource management diminished considerably. In the view of many analysts, the New Deal resource programs tended to be diverted from their original purpose to the dominant objectives of enhancing farm income and regulating production.

As environmental concerns and fears about resource exhaustion intensified in the 1970s, interest in agricultural conservation revived. The National Resources Inventory of 1977 revealed some important new facts. For example, soil erosion, though serious, is highly concentrated on a relatively small portion of agricultural land. The problem is at its worst in the Corn Belt and along the Mississippi River. Thus, present programs, which spread conservation efforts fairly evenly across the country, are unlikely to have the desired effect. (This mismatch is not accidental, but rather quite typical. Our political system tends to distribute benefits widely rather than concentrating them where they are most needed.)

An even more serious impediment to soil conservation is the influence of other government programs. As the Department of Agriculture acknowledges in a recently-released report:

> Export programs, target prices, price supports, production controls, Federal crop insurance, and Farmers Home Administration (FmHA) loans may create incentives to plant crops that encourage erosion. While programs may provide revenue for farmers to invest in conservation, the programs may create greater revenues for erosion than for conservation.

In short, other public goals, such as raising farm incomes, reducing risk, or boosting exports, may conflict with longterm soil conservation goals.

But the problem of soil erosion goes even deeper than the conflict between conservation and other programs. Studies indicate that in the short run, for the individual farmer, conservation simply does not pay. Longterm soil depletion is not adequately reflected in land prices, because private individuals give less weight than does society to the maintenance of our capacity to produce food in future generations. This is an important example of a phenomenon economists call "market failure," when the sum of individual decisions and transactions falls short of what is optimal for society as a whole. In all such cases, collective action—government regulation, subsidies, or other devices—is necessary to close the gap between private interests and the public good.

The issue of water conservation has arisen even more recently than that of soil conservation. Within the past few years, it has been recognized that total water consumption is outstripping supplies. Apart from specific regions, this does not yet pose an immediate national threat. But if current trends continue, it could be a major concern—even a crisis—by the turn of the century.

Agriculture is by far the largest user of water, requiring about 80 percent of total annual consumption. The scarcity of water has always been the major constraint on agriculture throughout the arid and semi-arid areas of the west and southwest. Starting in the early 1900s, the federal government has pursued massive water projects in these areas. It still spends $5 billion annually for these and related purposes.

This has led to a classic conflict between conservation and other goals. Water from federal projects has long been heavily subsidized, with the user paying only a fraction of the cost. This has promoted agricultural development in areas where it would not otherwise have occurred. But it has also encouraged highly inefficient irrigation that threatens in the long run to deplete water resources.

A related problem is the increasing pressure on groundwater. Although most of American agriculture still depends on rainfall, there is a growing amount of irrigation, much of it drawn from underground sources. The difficulty is that such sources tend to be renewed slowly if at all, while agriculture is tapping them at an accelerating rate. As a result, underground reserves are dropping dangerously. A particularly important example is the Ogallala aquifer, which lies beneath the plains states and portions of Texas. This aquifer supplies 25 percent of the total water needs for the irrigated farmland on which 12 percent of the nation's corn, cotton, sorghum, and wheat, and nearly one-half of our beef cattle, are produced. If current trends continue, substantial areas of this aquifer may be depleted and essentially unusable by the turn of the century.

The right to exploit water reserves has traditionally been part of that bundle of rights we call private property. But here, as in the case of soil erosion, the free market is sending signals to individuals the overall effect of which contradicts what society considers to be the most desirable long-term outcome. In short, there is a conflict between individual freedom and the well-being of the nation, including especially future generations who cannot yet make their wishes heard but who will be vitally affected by the choices we make today.

3. Farm Income and Structure

A third general goal that most Americans would assent to is this: Food and agriculture programs should be consistent with, and where possible promote, our shared conception of a community whose citizens enjoy equal opportunity and a reasonable level of protection against forces that are beyond their power to control. When applied to agricultural issues such as farm income and structure, however, the consensus over this goal gives way to complexities and disputes.

For example, many Americans believe that government policies should not serve to increase inequality of income, either within the class of program beneficiaries or between those who benefit from and those who pay for these programs. Other citizens believe equally firmly that such "distributional" concerns are irrelevant and even improper. This dispute bears directly on the evaluation of many current farm programs. Because most payments are based on acreage or production, farmers with very large incomes and asset bases receive on average far more than the smaller (and in most cases needier) farmers. (In 1983, the nation's 24,000 "super farms" with over $500,000 in annual sales received an average of $26,805 in direct government payments, while the smallest farms averaged $1,211). Similarly, a substantial portion of commodity program benefits flows from low and moderate-income taxpayers to wealthy commercial farmers.

Another frequently-invoked goal is the preservation of the rural way of life. As we have seen, the family farm occupies a unique place in our national culture. Today, as in Jefferson's time, politicians extol the independence, sense of community, moral virtue, and patriotism of family farmers. The shrinkage of this sector, it is alleged, diminishes opportunity, impoverishes our society, and even endangers our democracy. From this perspective, the family farm system should not be evaluated solely on grounds of economic efficiency. Its contribution to our country is beyond price, and we should all be willing to contribute to its rescue in time of need.

To evaluate this argument, it's important to be clear about what's really at stake. As we have seen, the percentage of Americans engaged in agricultural pursuits has shrunk almost continuously since the founding of our republic. Starting early in this century, the actual number of individuals began to shrink as well. Today, there are fewer than 700,000 units that match our rough conception of the "family farm." Of these, perhaps one-quarter to one-third are in serious difficulty. Even if all these endangered farms disappeared in the next few years, it is not clear that the moral character of our society would be crucially affected. (Discrete regions of the country would have to change, of course. But that is quite a different matter.)

There is a further difficulty. Analogous arguments can be made about many other sectors of the economy. Cities, states, even regions are heavily dependent on troubled industries. In many cases, generations have worked in the same steel mill, automobile plant, or coal mine. The shrinkage or total shut-down of these enterprises is more than an economic loss; it undermines communities. Does it follow that the government should intervene to protect them from change? For the most part, our collective answer has been negative. While we sympathize with the plight of affected families and frequently offer transition assistance, we have as a society rejected the proposition that inherited economic structures are to be propped up. Instead, we have placed our bets on dynamism and change. The extraordinary economic turnaround experienced by states that, like Massachusetts, accepted the inevitability of change and harnessed themselves to the future, is a leading example of this tendency. Thus, those who wish to preserve endangered family farms assume a considerable burden of proof. They must distinguish this sector from others with apparently comparable claims. And they must make plausible their contention that the intangible benefits of their proposal exceed its highly tangible costs.

There is a final argument. Most Americans believe that fellow-citizens have certain basic responsibilities to one another. In particular, when individuals are suffering through no fault of their own, the rest of us have a duty to do what is possible to help them. Hurricanes, droughts, floods—these and other natural disasters call for, and evoke, a response from the rest of the community. If so, many wonder, why shouldn't we also get together to help the victims of man-made catastrophes?

The issue then becomes: Whose errors produced the current plight of suffering farmers? The farmers blame the government. Economic policies that devalued the dollar contributed to the export boom of the 1970s. Government policy encouraged full production and made cheap credit readily available to farmers. Then the grain embargo and tight money hit agriculture a body-blow. Farmers who had borrowed heavily to expand and modernize their operations found themselves saddled with large debt and soaring real interest rates even as commodity prices and land values were falling sharply. Because the government sent farmers misleading signals for a full decade, it is now the government's responsibility to assist the victims of its folly.

The counterargument is that all Americans were in the same boat, making economic decisions in the context of high inflation, low real interest rates, and surging property values. Farmers and lenders assumed an investment risk that didn't pan out. But so did millions of others who bought real estate at its peak or took on heavy debt on the assumption that inflation would continue unabated. As OMB Director David Stockman put it in testimony before Congress, these were "transactions between consenting adults." The economy didn't force anyone to enter into them. Individuals are responsible for the choices they make within an overall economy for which they are not responsible. Only if there is no choice that wards off disaster (as was the case for so many during the Great Depression) should the government intervene. In the case of debt-ridden farmers, this condition is clearly not satisfied.

This is an example of how a shared moral premise ("Government should help innocent victims") can lead to a wide range of conclusions if, as is usually the case, there are differing interpretations of historical or other facts. But there is a very different premise on the basis of which proposed assistance to farmers can be evaluated—namely, economic efficiency.

4. Economic Growth and Competitiveness

Most Americans would agree that our agricultural programs should at least be consistent with the goals of overall economic growth and competitiveness in world markets. If they are not, then resources are being misallocated to agriculture when more national wealth could be produced by using those resources in some other manner.

From an economic standpoint, a key measure is the return investments can earn in different sectors of the economy. Returns higher than those available in other industries should signal additional investment, while lower returns ought to induce disinvestment.

As we have seen, while returns from agriculture over the long-term have closely paralleled those from other investments, they have been far smaller in the past four years. This suggests that one of two things must happen: either commodity prices must rise sharply to justify current prices for land and other assets, or asset values must decline to a level that can be supported by cash receipts. Few expect the former to occur, which suggests that the latter is virtually inevitable.

The question is, Who will bear the burden of declining farm assets? In the absence of government action, the burden will be divided in some manner between farmers driven into bankruptcy and banks forced to write down or write off bad loans. The economic argument for government action must be that the costs to society of non-intervention will exceed the costs of burden-sharing. This might be the case if, for example, widespread farm foreclosures led to bank failures and sharply depressed general economic activity throughout the farm belt—a possibility that cannot be dismissed out of hand.

This situation is hardly unparalleled. In the late 1970s, for example, the Chrysler Corporation was on the verge of bankruptcy. Some argued that it was a victim of its own mistakes and should be allowed to go under. Others, while conceding this point, replied that Chrysler's demise would mean the loss of half a million jobs that depended on Chrysler and serious economic reverses in many communities. The latter argument carried the day. The government stepped in with loans and loan guarantees, contingent on improved management and efficiency on the part of Chrysler. The plan worked—so quickly, in fact, that the public investment was repaid, with interest, well ahead of schedule.

This success story in no way proves that a farm bailout ought to be undertaken, or that it will succeed. But it does point to three important lessons. First, aid should be given only when there is a reasonable chance that the beneficiaries will eventually be able to make it on their own. The public has nothing to gain from a permanent bailout. Second, public aid ought to be given only in return for the kinds of changes in behavior that are needed to restore economic health to beneficiaries. And third, aid should be linked to some mechanism that will allow the public as well as direct beneficiaries to profit from a successful intervention into the marketplace. (In Chapter 5, we will examine the origin and dimensions of the farm credit crisis and evaluate options for dealing with it in light of the Chrysler lessons.)

Beyond the immediate farm credit crisis, the goals of growth, efficiency, and competitiveness raise a number of other important issues.

Economists argue that these goals are best achieved when many different producers, none of which dominates the market, are competing against one another to offer the best product at the lowest price. Some advocates of the family farm have seized on this, contending that the current crisis will lead to consolidation that concentrates production in so few hands that prices can be fixed. At present, this fear seems far-fetched. A shift from 600,000 producers to 600 might have this effect. A shift from 600,000 to 400,000 (the worst-case outcome of the current crisis) will certainly not. In fact, it would probably have no effect whatever on competition or prices.

A related concern is the impact of public policy on farm size. Some argue that the trend toward concentration is not the product of "natural" forces but results, directly or indirectly, from political decisions. For example, programs that give greater benefits to larger than to smaller producers only increase the edge larger producers already enjoy. Investments in new products or processes may alter the relation between farm size and the optimal cost of production. Economic policies that increase instability give the advantage to larger units that have the cash and other reserves needed to survive abrupt downturns.

The issue of instability is not new. Since antiquity, it has been recognized that agriculture must contend with unpredictable forces of nature, weather, infestation, and disease. Because production is biological, it cannot be regulated like an industrial process. And the farmer's ability to respond flexibly to changing conditions is limited. Most inputs are fully committed at the beginning of the season, growth requires a lengthy period of time, and the output becomes available on the market all at once.

This natural instability of agriculture has been increased in recent decades by two other developments. As agriculture has become more capital-intensive and dependent on credit, it has become more vulnerable to the vagaries of national economic policy, which produce significant swings in the quantity and price of borrowed money. And as agriculture has become more dependent on exports, it has become more sensitive to national policies that affect currency exchange rates, export competitiveness, interest rates on international loans, and world growth rates, particularly in developing countries. For example, the 20 percent rise in the value of the dollar in 1981 and 1982, resulting largely from the American budget deficit and high real interest rates, reduced exports of corn, wheat, and soybeans by $3 billion. Each added percentage point in interest rates costs developing countries (our major export growth market during the 1970s) $4 billion, reducing their ability to import.

Increased export dependence also increases our exposure to variations in the world market. These variations can be extreme. Only 9 percent of world production is traded, and relatively small changes in production or consumption can have large effects. For example, when the Soviet Union imported 23 million tons of grain (a tiny fraction of world production) in 1973, prices surged.

Government policies magnify the instability. Sudden buying decisions by foreign governments or embargoes by our own lead to abrupt shifts in demand. Policies (such as those of the Common Market and Japan) that insulate consumers and producers from world market prices force consumers and producers elsewhere to bear the burden of adjustment. The United States has often borne a disproportionate share, expanding or contracting production in response to changing conditions. The effects of this trade-induced instability ripple through the entire agricultural economy and in-

29

fluence the trade balance and budget deficit as well.

To be sure, some instability has been reduced in recent times. Technological advances have greatly reduced risks from diseases and pests. Plant and animal breeding has increased resistance to weather variations. Better machinery has reduced planting and harvest time. Federally-subsidized crop insurance is now widely available. Improved futures and options markets allow farmers to lock in prices well before harvest and to share the risk of fluctuations with purchasers. Nevertheless, it is clear that, on balance, instability has increased markedly in the past decade. This development has had a number of undesirable consequences: windfall profits and undeserved losses; misallocation of resources; painful adjustments for farmers; and huge and continuing costs for taxpayers.

Most experts agree that reducing instability is a major justification for government intervention in agriculture in the 1980s and beyond. But there the consensus ends. Some believe that the only way to do this is to detach ourselves from the prime source of instability—dependence on foreign markets. Others believe that we should seek to transform the impact of export dependence by abandoning domestic policies that reduce our flexibility while pressing other nations to discard the practices that have imposed such large burdens on the United States. Either course would imply a very significant departure from current arrangements.

5. Foreign Responsibilities

Most Americans would agree that American agriculture should, where possible, make a positive contribution to other peoples and nations. The spontaneous public response to starvation in Africa shows clearly that our sense of responsibility and humanitarianism in no way stops at our national border.

The role of the United States in assuring adequate worldwide food supplies has expanded considerably in recent years. Developing countries have increased their dependence on food imports by more than half since 1970. For some, it is the difference between life and death. In the immediate future, eight drought-stricken countries in southern Africa will rely on outside sources for 66 percent of their grains and 14 percent of their total food supply. And because such countries typically cannot buy adequate quantities at market prices, concessional pricing and outright donations are critical. The actions of the United States, which provides well over one-half of the world's food aid, are of extreme importance in such emergency situations.

The United States also plays a crucial role in providing world food security, primarily through its reserve policies. When global production falls below the requirements of consumption, hunger and starvation can be avoided only by dipping into food reserves. The United States holds a large share of the world's reserves and tends to absorb most of the needed adjustments—over 60 percent in the troubled years of the early 1970s.

Our world responsibilities have led to many complications and perplexities. For example, attempts to raise farm incomes through price supports reduce our capacity to export, decrease the access of poor nations to our food supplies, and increase the cost of food aid.

Beyond this is the fact, more widely recognized today than a generation ago, that the key problems are not so much overall food supplies as poverty and dependence. The long-term solution lies, not in the United States feeding more and more people, but in helping other nations increase their purchasing power and produce more of their own food.

This is no simple matter. Short-term American aid can actually impede progress toward long-term independence. Flooding local markets with cheap imported food may depress local farm prices and reduce production. The availability of concessional food imports may make it easier for developing countries to ignore agricultural development by persisting in policies that subsidize urban food and eliminate incentives for farmers to increase production. Food aid can have other adverse effects as well. It may compete with local production for scarce transportation, storage, handling, financing, and communications. And it may hinder the development of marketing channels for domestically produced food. In short, unless informed by clear-eyed realism, our humanitarian impulses can actually harm the intended beneficiaries of our good will.

But it is important not to carry this conclusion to extremes. Much depends on the policies of recipient governments—on how the aid is administered and for what it is used. A government intent upon improving agricultural production but facing strong political pressures to keep food prices low may use food aid to stabilize costs to consumers while paying farmers higher prices. For example, it is quite possible that one of the great success stories, India, would not have been able to move from repeated famine to self-sufficiency in food production without the massive food aid it received in the 1960s.

The same holds true for broader development policies. In past decades, a heavy emphasis on large infrastructure projects (roads, bridges, dams) diverted local resources in developing countries away from their domestic agriculture. And aid directly to or through governments may have encouraged bureaucratic control of economic activity, frequently to the detriment of agriculture. On the other hand, some governments have tried to develop their infrastructure in a way that promotes the efficient production and transportation of agricultural products.

American agricultural interests sometimes object that development aid for foreign agriculture undermines our national well-being by encouraging production that competes with our products. Fortunately, in a policy arena that (as we have seen) is full of contradictory goals, this particular concern appears to be exaggerated. On balance, expanding production in other nations increases their purchasing power and adds to demand for our products.

American agriculture does best when world purchasing power is increasing briskly. This will require, not just targeted development assistance, but also economic policies that are consistent with global growth. American budget deficits suck in capital needed by other nations and export high interest rates. In the international sphere as well as domestically, the resolution of our fiscal troubles may well be a prerequisite to the success of other policies.

Means

Finally, let us look briefly at the debate about appropriate means to employ in implementing agricultural policy.

There are two basic issues: How much? and What kind?

As we have seen, the soaring costs of current farm programs have been a major stimulus for reconsidering them. But how much is too much? One way to look at this question is to compare the costs of doing less (or nothing at all) to the costs of present policies. This requires a complex and inherently controversial prediction about the effects of federal government retrenchment in this area. Some argue that diminished intervention will produce a rash of rural bank failures, a depression throughout rural America, and a significant increase in poverty and unemployment—all of which will require higher social expenditures. Others argue that these purported consequences are highly exaggerated for political effect.

A deeper difficulty arises when we compare, not the dollar costs of two different courses of action, but dollars against intangibles. How much (if anything) is it worth to us to keep farmers on the land their families have farmed for generations? How much do we, or should we, care about rising rates of alcoholism, child abuse, mental illness, and suicide that accompany rural distress?

The second basic issue—What kind of means?—has been much in the news lately. Some advocates of the free market argue that it is immoral to use the coercive power of government to transfer wealth from one individual or group of individuals to another. Others argue that such transfers are perfectly proper. They are said to reflect the fact that as fellow-citizens, we are members of a single community (some have even called it a family) and that we should therefore be willing to share the burdens as well as benefits of our collective existence.

A related issue first arose during the Great Depression and has reemerged today: Even if we could raise farm incomes by directly telling farmers as individuals how much of each kind of crop they were allowed to plant, would that be the right thing to do? Would it be consistent with our beliefs about individual liberty and the proper role of government?

These and similar moral questions cannot be answered easily. But as the evaluation of radically divergent solutions now offered for the rural crisis proceeds, neither we nor our elected representatives will be altogether able to avoid them.

SELECTED REFERENCES

American Farmland Trust, *Soil Conservation in America: What Do We Have to Lose?*, 1984.

Sandra S. Batie, ''Agricultural Policy and Soil Conservation: Implications for the 1985 Farm Bill.'' American Enterprise Institute Occasional Paper, December 1984.

Committee on Agriculture, Nutrition, and Forestry, United States Senate, *Food Safety: Where Are We?*, July 1979.

Food Research and Action Council and National Anti-Hunger Coalition, *Hunger in the Eighties: A Primer,* 1984.

Thomas A. Miller, *Increasing World Market Fluctuations and U.S. Agriculture: A Summary of Implications.* Economic Research Service, USDA, October 1984.

Jerry A. Sharples, Alan Webb, and Forrest Holland, *World Trade and U.S. Farm Policy.* Economic Research Service, USDA, June 1984.

Luther Tweeten, *Causes and Consequences of Structural Change in the Farm Industry.* National Planning Association, 1984.

Winrock International, *World Agriculture: Review and Prospects in the 1990s,* December 1983.

Section II

The Economic Context of the Debate

The purpose of Section II is to discuss three key problems, not addressed in the traditional quadrennial "farm bill," that are helping to create the economic context for current debate over agricultural policy.

Chapter 3 discusses the impact of federal macroeconomic policy on agriculture and explores the consequences of altering monetary policy and cutting the budget deficit substantially from current levels.

Chapter 4 discusses the impact of federal tax policy on agriculture and explores the consequences of various tax reform proposals now under consideration.

Chapter 5 discusses the most severe short-term difficulty facing American agriculture—the inability of many farmers to repay the large debts they incurred during the boom years of the 1970s. This chapter explains the origins and dimensions of the farm credit crisis and explores some options for addressing it.

Chapter 3

Macroeconomic Policy and Agriculture

Macroeconomic policy has two major components—shaping the budget of the federal government and managing the nation's money supply. The budget is a joint product of the executive branch and the Congress, while monetary policy is the province of the Federal Reserve Board, a powerful and independent agency. The interaction between the budget and the money supply is one of the most important determinants of inflation, interest rates, overall levels of economic growth, and the distribution of that growth among different sectors of the economy.

Agriculture is now unusually sensitive to macroeconomic policy. Interest rates are the key link. Agriculture is one of the most credit-intensive areas of the economy. At the end of 1984, farmers owed more than $210 billion and paid $22 billion annually in interest on that debt. A one point change in the average interest rate on farm debt means about a $2 billion change in annual farm production costs. And in the same way that rising mortgage rates tend to hold down the value of housing, increasing interest burdens depress the value of farmers' major asset—their land.

A key measure of the pressure exerted by interest payments is the so-called "real" interest rate—that is, the difference between the rate actually paid (the "nominal" rate) and the rate of inflation. During much of the 1970s, when interest rates were rising, inflation was rising even more rapidly. As a result, real interest rates fell and even turned negative for a time, as the rate of inflation exceeded the nominal rate of interest. Not surprisingly, the entire economy, including agriculture, went on a borrowing binge.

By late 1979, inflation had become intolerable, and the Federal Reserve Board shifted its monetary policy dramatically. Rather than focusing on making credit affordable, the Fed clamped down on credit in an effort to curb the inflationary spiral. At roughly the same time, the federal budget deficit began to surge, from $29 billion in 1979, to nearly $60 billion in 1980, to more than $100 billion in 1981, to roughly $200 billion in each of the past three years. The collision between tight money and a loose budget, which required the government to borrow huge sums each year, drove the real cost of money up sharply. By 1984, real interest rates were 8 to 10 percent—four to five times their historical level. This development created serious stresses throughout our economy, nowhere more severe than in agriculture. The sector was plunged into a credit crisis (discussed in detail in Chapter 5) that threatens to drive tens or even hundreds of thousands of farmers off their land in the next few years.

Beyond these direct effects, interest rates indirectly affect another area of critical importance to agriculture—exports.

High real interest rates help attract foreign capital to the United States. Because other currencies must be converted into dollars before they can be invested here, this capital influx increases demand for the dollar, raising its value (the "exchange rate") in relation to foreign currencies. The higher value of the dollar makes U. S. goods more expensive to overseas buyers, reducing exports.

High real interest rates also impose huge burdens on the most rapidly growing markets for U. S. products—the developing countries. During the 1970s, when the real interest rate was low or even negative, these countries borrowed heavily to finance rapid growth. The resulting surge in income and purchasing power enabled them to upgrade the living standards of their populations by multiplying their purchases of U. S. goods. (By the end of the decade, developing countries accounted for 40 percent of all U. S. agricultural exports.) But in the 1980s, high real interest rates have forced them to devote a much higher proportion of their GNP to the servicing of their international debt, reducing their ability to import. The need to earn foreign currency by showing positive balances of trade has only made matters worse, because this goal cannot be achieved without restricting imports.

This sequence of events has hit agriculture with particular force. Agriculture is one of the most export-dependent sectors of our economy. Nearly 40 percent of all planted acres in this country produce for foreign consumption, and exports represent more than one third of total farm sales. Between 1970 and 1981, U. S. agricultural exports rose almost six-fold, from $7.3 billion to $43.8 billion. But since then, exports have fallen by about 20 percent.

Largely in response, commodity prices have sagged, and net farm income has followed suit. In real terms, net farm income is scarcely higher today than it was at the end of the Great Depression.

The precise quantitative relations between macroeconomic policy and the performance of agriculture cannot be known with certainty. Nevertheless, certain approximations are widely accepted:

(1) Each $50 billion cut in the U. S. budget deficit would reduce real interest rates by 1 to 2 points.

(2) Each 1 point reduction in interest rates would reduce annual interest costs on farm debt by $2 billion.

(3) Each 1 point reduction in real interest rates would lower value of the dollar by 5 to 10 percent.

(4) Each 1 percent drop in the value of the dollar would eventually increase farm exports by 0.5 to 1 percent.

(5) Each 1 percent increase in farm exports would increase net farm income by 0.25 percent.

Thus, cutting the federal budget deficit by about $150 billion between now and 1989 (a target recommended by most economists and broadly accepted in the Congress) would increase net farm income by anywhere from 25 to 60 percent—$6.4 to $15.4 billion—annually. As we shall see (Chapters 6 to 9), this is a far greater gain than could be expected from any program targeted directly to agriculture. For this reason, the frequently-articulated proposition that in the long run, cutting the federal budget deficit is the most important thing our policy-makers can do for farmers would seem to be supported by the available evidence.

The budget deficit is, however, only half the story. It is the interaction between the budget and monetary policy that creates the environment within which agriculture and the rest of the economy must function.

Recently, two professors of agricultural economics, Dean W. Hughes and John B. Penson Jr., have attempted to project the consequences for agriculture of three different fiscal-monetary scenarios. Under the first (S1), no effective action is taken between now and the end of the decade to cut the federal budget deficit, and the Federal Reserve Board continues to respond with a tight-money, anti-inflationary policy. Under the second (S2), the budget deficit also remains at roughly current levels, but the Fed attempts to reduce interest rates by supplying credit to the economy at a more rapid pace, even at the risk of rekindling inflation. Under the third (S3), the budget deficit is reduced by about 15 percent a year, cutting the deficit from a projected $260 billion in 1989 to only $115 billion, and monetary policy is enabled to pursue a moderate-growth, low-inflation path.

The outcome of these three policies for agriculture is instructive.

Table 1.
Real Long-Term Interest Rates

	1985	1986	1987	1988	1989
	— — — percent — — —				
S1	8.6	8.8	9.0	9.0	9.0
S2	2.9	3.0	3.2	3.4	3.6
S3	8.0	7.7	7.5	7.3	7.1

Table 2.
Real Farm Asset Values

	1985	1986	1987	1988	1989
		——billion 1967 dollars——			
S1	339.8	332.6	322.7	310.9	296.8
S2	357.9	358.1	348.4	331.6	314.4
S3	374.5	396.7	413.3	425.3	436.7

Table 3.
Real Net Farm Income

	1985	1986	1987	1988	1989
		——billion 1967 dollars——			
S1	5.0	9.7	11.8	7.7	8.1
S2	10.9	12.5	10.6	6.5	4.4
S3	12.4	16.2	15.7	13.7	13.1

The major conclusions are clear. The continuation of the current mix, high budget deficits coupled with tight money, holds out no hope of reducing real interest rates or raising real farm income from its current low level. But the oft-proposed remedy, looser money, provides no long-term relief either. After falling dramatically in the wake of this policy change, real interest rates would begin to rise again. After increasing early on, real asset values and farm income would begin to fall rapidly. By 1989, farm income would be even lower than under current policy. In short, this forecast reinforces the major lessons of the 1970s for agriculture: Inflation is not an adequate long-term policy for the sector.

The only macroeconomic policy that offers the prospect of steady, long-term declines in real interest rates and increases in assets and income is S3—a tighter budget that would permit a somewhat more relaxed monetary policy. Under S3, real farm income between 1986 and 1989 would average $14.7 billion, almost 60 percent higher than under current policies, while assets would be almost 45 percent higher by the end of the four-year period.

Of course, achieving an overall deficit reduction of more than 50 percent over four years would probably require some significant cuts in current farm programs (the Hughes-Penson calculations assume no changes in these programs). But even if the programs were eliminated altogether (an unlikely outcome), net farm income would be substantially greater than under the current regime of relatively generous targeted programs and highly unfavorable macroeconomic policies.

SELECTED REFERENCES

Dean W. Hughes and John B. Penson, Jr., ''Financial Conditions in the Farm Sector 1984-1990: Projections for Different Macroeconomic Policies.'' Thornton Agricultural Finance Institute Research Working Paper, October 1984.

John Lee, ''Macroeconomic Policy and Agriculture.'' Conference on Agricultural Debt and Finance, November 1984.

Gordon C. Rausser, ''Macroeconomics and U.S. Agricultural Policy.'' Giannini Foundation of Agricultural Economics, University of California, January 1985.

Chapter 4

Tax Policy and Agriculture

Introduction

In recent years, federal tax policy has become increasingly controversial. Two questions figure most prominently in the debate. First, what should be the overall level of federal taxation? This was a major issue in the 1984 election. Walter Mondale contended that the budget deficit could not be adequately reduced without a substantial tax increase. President Reagan replied that some combination of economic growth and spending cuts could do the job and that new revenues would only be devoured by new programs. As the debate over the 1986 budget intensifies, this issue may well re-emerge. (It is already a matter of discussion within as well as between the two major political parties.)

The second key question concerns, not the overall *level* of tax revenues, but rather their *source*. Over the past decade, economists, politicians, businesspeople, and average citizens have become increasingly aware of the ways in which different kinds of taxes can create incentives or disincentives to engage in particular activities. During this period, the federal tax structure—especially the income tax—has become much more complex. Congress has enacted hundreds of special tax credits and deductions, purportedly to encourage certain activities, promote public policy goals, and recognize special hardship or need. Many of these provisions have been attacked on the ground that they serve narrow interests and seriously distort the economy. Leading legislators in both political parties have offered sweeping tax simplification proposals that would wipe out most of these provisions. The decision of the President to weigh in on the side of tax simplification virtually ensures that a major debate on the issue will occur in 1985 or early 1986.

Agriculture is affected by both these dimensions of tax policy. As we saw in Chapter 3, agriculture is unusually sensitive to the federal budget deficit and will feel the long-term effects of the decision to include or exclude added tax revenues from deficit reduction strategies. In addition, agriculture is affected to a considerable degree by the structure of the federal tax code.

43

Although the size of the impact is difficult to measure, most experts believe that special tax provisions affect farm size, land prices, management practices, and even commodity prices. The purpose of this chapter is to sketch some of these key provisions and to show how they help structure the agricultural economy.

Key Provisions

1. Cash accounting

For income tax purposes, most businesses are required to use what is known as "accrual accounting." Under this system, the costs of producing goods are not deducted from the taxpayer's gross income until the year these goods are actually sold. Farmers, on the other hand, are allowed to use "cash accounting," which permits expenses to be deducted before income from sales is received. Farmers can therefore reduce their overall taxes by shifting expenses to high income years, or vice versa—for example, by prepaying certain production costs.

2. Depreciation

Not all business expenses are deductible in the year they are incurred. Investments in such long-lived assets as machinery and buildings are "depreciated." That is, a portion of their total cost is written off in each year of the period the tax code defines as the "useful life" of the asset. The shorter that period, the greater the advantage to the business.

The Economic Recovery Tax Act of 1981 established the so-called Accelerated Cost Recovery System (ACRS), which significantly shortened depreciation schedules. Most businesses benefitted, farms among them. For example, breeding hogs were deemed to have a useful life of only three years. Most farm machinery and equipment, breeding livestock other than hogs, and production and storage facilities were awarded a useful life of only five years. These periods are much shorter than the actual life of such assets. Thus, they can contribute to farm income long after they have been fully depreciated, exaggerating the mismatch between income and expenses discussed above. In addition, generous depreciation rules increase incentives to make capital investments that would not otherwise be economically justifiable.

3. Investment Tax Credit

More than two decades ago, in an effort to spur what was believed to be lagging investment by business, the federal government established the investment tax credit (ITC). This provision allows taxpayers to reduce their tax liability by a certain amount (now 10 percent of "eligible costs"—usually the purchase price) in the year assets are acquired.

Most depreciable farm property—machinery, livestock, fences and storage facilities, and single-purpose structures—qualifies for the ITC. When combined with accelerated depreciation, the ITC provides a powerful incentive for overall farm investment and tends to skew that investment in certain directions. For example, the special status of single-purpose facilities such as hog confinement facilities and milking barns undoubtedly increases the flow of funds into these activities, raising production and depressing prices.

4. Capital Gains

The federal tax code distinguishes between two broad classes of assets: property held or used for sale in a business; and property used as an investment or to produce and conduct a business. Items in the second category are known as "capital assets," and income from their sale is known as "capital gains." While ordinary income is taxed at rates up to 50 percent, capital gains are taxed at a maximum rate of 20 percent. Thus, it is highly advantageous for taxpayers to be able to classify the largest possible fraction of their income as capital gains, and considerable effort is devoted to this objective. Correspondingly, the prices of capital assets are bid up relative to other assets because investors are primarily concerned about post-tax income.

The key agricultural input—farmland—is treated as a capital asset. Most agricultural crops or products raised for sale are not considered capital assets, and proceeds from their sale are taxed as ordinary income. But livestock raised for breeding purposes and held for at least a year qualify as capital assets, as do livestock held for dairy or sporting purposes. These special provisions tend to increase the flow of investment into such areas as dairy cattle and racehorses. They also affect management practices. For example, to raise the fraction of their income classified as capital gains, hog farmers tend to sell their sows after only one litter, even though the average quality of their offspring would be improved if they were held for three or four litters.

5. Employment Taxes

Many farmers who have employees must pay employer-employee taxes. For social security purposes, farmers must withhold roughly 7 percent of employee salaries and contribute an equal amount as their employer's share. Farmers who pay wages of $20,000 or employ at least 10 farmworkers for an appreciable fraction of the tax year must pay a federal unemployment tax of 3.5 percent of the first $7,000 of wages paid to each employee. By law, this tax cannot be deducted or collected from employee wages.

The contrast between the tax treatment of labor and that accorded capital is dramatic. In effect, farmers are penalized for hiring employees, while recent changes in the tax code have increased incentives for capital investments. As a result, farming is almost certainly more capital-intensive than it would be with a more neutral tax code. (In this regard, of course, agriculture is much like the rest of our economy.)

Effects of the Tax Code

1. Tax Shelters

A tax shelter has been defined as an investment that allows certain taxpayers to reduce or even eliminate taxes they would otherwise owe by making use of special provisions of the tax code. In general, the advantages of shelters are restricted to taxpayers with large incomes potentially taxable at high rates.

A recent study identifies four income tax provisions that make farming an attractive shelter:

1. cash accounting, which permits advantageous timing of expenses and income;

2. deductibility of many capital expenditures;

3. farm asset depreciation schedules that are much shorter than their actual economically useful lives; and

4. favorable capital gains treatment of many farm assets.

These advantages are available to high-income farmers as well as wealthy non-farmers drawn to agriculture as a tax investment.

The attractiveness of farming as a tax shelter has three important consequences.

First, the federal government suffers a significant revenue loss—estimated at between $1 and $1.5 billion annually—which either widens the budget deficit or imposes added burdens on average taxpayers.

Second, new money continues to flow into agriculture at a time when existing producers are already suffering from excess capacity and low prices.

Third, because high-income taxpayers are willing to accept low or even negative returns from farming operations when coupled with large tax advantages, excessive rates of investment and production are induced, reducing the rate of return from operations for all farmers. This imposes a special burden on mid-sized family farmers who depend almost exclusively on the return they can earn from raising and selling commodities. To put the same point slightly differently: Family farmers in relatively low tax brackets lose more in reduced commodity prices than they gain from the tax advantages. For higher bracket taxpayers (corporate farmers or investors), the reverse is true.

2. Other effects

Beyond the effects already discussed, the tax code tends to affect the structure of agriculture through its impact on land values and operating efficiencies.

Land values. The treatment of land as a capital asset, coupled with other features of the tax code such as the deductibility of interest costs on loans to purchase land and the deductibility of property taxes, has tended to bid up land values, especially in times when inflation is high and cash returns from operations are relatively low. This favors high-income, established farmers and wealthy non-farm investors over small and beginning farmers. Conversely, when inflationary expectations are reduced, demand for farmland falls much faster than does farm income, and values collapse. (This is the sequence we have seen in the 1970s and early 1980s.) In short, the tax code increases instability by exaggerating both upswings and downturns in land values. And instability works against mid-sized producers, particularly younger farmers who are more dependent on debt secured by farmland as collateral.

Operating efficiencies. By subsidizing capital investment so heavily, depreciation and other features of the tax code tilt the economic playing field in favor of the largest producers who can maximize the use of new facilities and equipment, thereby reducing production costs per unit. This tendency is particularly pronounced in the hog industry, which received significant new tax breaks under ACRS. A recent study has found that wealthy farmers and investors in the highest tax bracket benefitted three times as much from these changes as did small farmers in the average tax bracket. Between 1980 and the present, more than 30 percent of all hog producers, most of them small and mid-sized operators, have gone out of business. At the same time, six major corporations have announced expansion plans that will add significantly to annual hog production, depressing prices. Smaller hog farmers who are already operating at the margin will be forced out, accelerating the process of concentration. Other agricultural industries similarly affected by the tax code include poultry growing and cattle feeding.

Conclusion: Options for Tax Reform

As we have seen, some of the key provisions of the current tax code have a significant—many would say distortive—effect on the conduct of the agricultural sector. Some of these provisions are being reconsidered as part of the burgeoning debate over fundamental tax reform. For example, there are efforts underway to modify ACRS if not eliminate it outright. The initial Treasury Department proposal went very far in that direction, and the follow-up proposal is likely to retain major, though perhaps less dramatic, changes. On the other hand, the key Republican congressional bill, Kemp-

47

Kasten, retains ACRS, while the key Democratic bill, Bradley-Gephardt, leaves agricultural depreciation virtually unchanged. In addition, there is growing support for a strengthened minimum tax, which would reduce the aggregate benefits individuals could reap from tax preferences. Finally, most parties to the debate agree that the revenue base should be broadened in return for reductions in tax rates. These moves would also reduce the attractiveness of shelters.

Other key features of the code appear less amenable to change. For example, shifting from cash to accrual accounting would bar many tax-motivated decisions, but it would also impose significant record-keeping and accounting costs which would fall most heavily on small and mid-sized farmers who cannot afford professional tax assistance. Closing the gap between capital gains and ordinary income would reduce the appeal of tax shelters, but it might also reduce the supply of venture capital, hindering risk-taking, entrepreneurship, and economic growth. And the systematic bias of the tax system against investment in labor cannot be corrected without major reductions in payroll taxes, which would threaten our national commitment to such programs as Social Security.

In all probability, the goal of a simple, neutral, fair system of taxaion could not be fully achieved, even if it were universally supported, which it isn't. Many of the distortions of the current system are the unintended consequences of decisions made for entirely different reasons. Given the complexity of the modern economy—including agriculture—reform measures will inevitably bring with them a number of surprises. The task of tax reform today is to deal with the most serious, distortive abuses in a manner well calculated to minimize the unpleasant side-effects of change. To the extent that this can be achieved, some of the forces accelerating the demise of family farms and the rise of concentrated corporate agriculture would be diminished, and the future structure of agriculture would be more nearly determined by true efficiencies of production.

SELECTED REFERENCES

Center for Rural Affairs, "Modified Flat Tax Proposals: Their Treatment of Agriculture and Impact on Family Farm Survival and Profitability."

Charles Davenport, Michael D. Boehlje, and David B.H. Martin, *The Effects of Tax Policy on American Agriculture*. Economic Research Service, USDA, February 1982.

Richard W. Dunford, *The Effects of Federal Income Tax Policy on U.S. Agriculture*. Joint Economic Committee, Congress of the United States, 1985.

Chapter 5

Farm Credit: Crisis and Options

Origin of the Credit Crisis

Today, tens of thousands of farmers are poised on the brink of bankruptcy, unable to repay their debts. Within two years, hundreds of thousands may well be driven off the land—the largest agricultural shakeout since the Great Depression.

The current farm financial crisis has its roots in the 1970s when, as we have seen, farmers responded aggressively to expanding exports, rising inflation, soaring land values, and low (sometimes negative) real interest rates. Many operators, among them some of the most enterprising and efficient, borrowed heavily, pledging their land as collateral. In 1971, total farm debt was about $54 billion. In 1976, it was $91 billion. By the early 1980s, it topped $200 billion. Today it is over $212 billion—a sum exceeding the combined foreign debt of Brazil, Mexico, and Argentina.

The major farm lenders are commercial banks, the Farm Credit System (which includes Federal Land Banks, Federal Intermediate Credit Banks, Production Credit Associations and the Central and District Banks for Cooperatives), the Farmers Home Administration, life insurance companies, the Commodity Credit Corporation, individuals and others. There are two main categories of farm debt: real estate loans, usually long-term and collateralized by land; and non-real estate loans, usually shorter term, undertaken to finance current operations or to survive disasters.

Forty-eight percent of farm debt is short-term, non-real estate debt that often must be paid off in five years or less. Fifty-two percent of all farm debt is longer term real estate debt, usually calling for retirement within 20 to 25 years.

Table 1.
Distribution of Farm Debt

Lender	Type of Debt		
	Real Estate	Nonreal Estate	TOTAL
	———million dollars———		
Commercial Banks	10,179	40,551	50,730
Farm Credit System	48,444	19,006	67,450
Federal Land Banks	48,444	—	48,444
Production Credit Associations	—	18,129	18,129
Federal Intermediate Credit Banks	—	877	877
Farmers Home Administration	9,956	15,206	25,162
Life Insurance Companies	12,375	—	12,375
Individuals and Others	29,900	18,200	48,100
Commodity Credit Corporation	—	8,312	8,312
TOTAL	110,854	101,275	212,129

Source: USDA, "The Current Financial Condition of Farmers and Farm Lenders," March 1985, p.22.

Farmers undertook this debt burden on the assumption that inflation would remain high, markets would continue to grow, and commodity prices and land values would keep rising. But by the end of 1979, inflation had become intolerable. The Federal Reserve Board shifted to a tight-money, anti-inflationary stance. The collision between this policy and rising U. S. budget deficits produced soaring real interest rates, which hit American agriculture with cataclysmic force.

Three effects were of particular importance.

First, as high interest rates sent the world economy into recession and distorted the value of the dollar, exports collapsed. During this same period, net farm income fell by nearly one-half, and by 1983 real (inflation-corrected) farm income reached its lowest level since 1940.

Second, as inflation cooled, real long-term interest rates soared from about 2 percent to almost 10 percent, greatly increasing the interest burden on debt-ridden farmers.

Third, the value of the land used to support this debt contracted dramatically. For the first time since the Great Depression, the average value of farmland has fallen for four consecutive years. Nationwide, the decline is about 10 percent from the 1980 peak. In some parts of the Midwest, the decline is approaching 40 percent.

Dimensions of the Problem

These developments have imperiled farmers, lenders, and the entire agricultural sector.

Today, more than one-quarter of all farmers are experiencing serious financial stress. More than 10 percent have debt-to-asset ratios that will make survival for more than another two years virtually impossible. 43,000 family-size commercial farmers are already insolvent—that is, owe more than the value of their assets. Up to 65 percent of all farm debt—$130 billion—is in some degree of jeopardy, and writeoffs of $20 billion now seem all but inevitable.

In analyzing troubled loans, economists typically distinguish between "liquidity" and "solvency" problems. Liquidity is at issue when a borrower who has enough assets to support his loan temporarily lacks the cash to repay the principal and interest on schedule. Solvency is at issue when the borrower cannot service the loan because of long-term declines in asset values or cash flow. The standard remedy for a liquidity problem is a short-term additional loan or postponement of repayment sufficient to get the borrower over the difficult period, at which time the original terms of the loan are reinstated. The remedy for a solvency problem, on the other hand, involves some long-term adjustment in the terms of the loan or in the asset-to-liability structure of the debtor. (The alternative to adjustment is default or foreclosure.)

The evidence is overwhelming that although a number of fundamentally sound farmers are experiencing a liquidity squeeze, the agricultural credit crisis is primarily one of solvency. Under current circumstances, most endangered farmers have neither adequate cash-flow to service their loans nor adequate collateral (pledged assets, usually land) to support them. And without a sharp upturn in the agricultural economy, these problems will continue.

Agricultural creditors have been gravely affected. Loan delinquencies and writeoffs have soared at Federal Land Banks and Production Credit Associations. More than 25 percent of all FmHA debt is now behind schedule. And a number of the 4100 commercial banks heavily committed to agricultural loans may go under. Between 1982 and 1984, the percentage of farm banks officially classified as "problem" banks more than doubled, from 13 percent to 27 percent. Agricultural banks now account for 37 percent of all problem banks. And the pace of farm bank failures is accelerating. In 1983, farm banks accounted for 13 percent of all bank failures. For 1984, the figure was 32 percent. For the last quarter of 1984, it was 61 percent.

The average agricultural bank has very little room to maneuver. If 10 percent of its loans are classified as uncollectable, its working capital may well be driven below the legal requirement, forcing regulators to step in and shut its doors. (As we have seen, 10 percent is a very modest estimate of potential loan losses in this sector.)

Options

Beginning in September of 1984, the Reagan administration has gradually expanded access to farm credit. The FmHA has been empowered to defer a portion of principal and interest payments on its direct loans and to extend guarantees on restructured loans that meet certain requirements.

In March, 1985, Congress sent to the President legislation that represented a significant further liberalization of credit. This bill would have raised the authorized level of federal loan guarantees by $1.85 billion; appropriated $100 million to buy down interest rates on farm loans; and advanced a portion of price-support loans, usually paid out after crops are harvested, to farmers who now have no other source of operating capital for their spring planting. Arguing that existing programs were adequate for needy farmers and that further efforts would only bust the budget, President Reagan vetoed the bill.

If the administration's credit program proves adequate to achieve widely supported public goals, this issue will subside. But if the administration's program comes to be perceived as inadequate, proposals for more extensive credit relief are likely to resurface. Some of these proposals could have a direct impact on the shape of the 1985 farm bill.

There are three basic strategies that further credit assistance to farmers could employ.

1. Increase Farm Income

First, farm incomes could be raised through transfers to producers, in the form of either higher price supports or more rigorous production controls. This strategy could yield a number of immediate benefits. It would enable some endangered farmers to make the payments on their loans. It would slow the concentration of land ownership. And to the extent that it were perceived as a long-term commitment, it would halt the erosion of land values by increasing the projected income-stream that helps determine those values.

This strategy also has a number of disadvantages. Direct transfers would run into many billions of dollars, at a time when cutting the budget deficit is probably our most urgent domestic priority. If added agricultural expenditures contributed significantly to the collapse of broader efforts to move toward budgetary balance, short-term benefits to farmers would be swamped by the adverse long-term effects of continued high interest rates and a strong dollar. The other means of raising farm incomes—stringent production controls—would spur inflation by radically increasing farm prices and would further reduce the competitiveness of our exports in world markets. (A recent USDA study indicates that commodity prices would have to rise by 32 percent to restore the profitability of endangered family-size commercial farms.) Both of these measures would confer benefits indiscriminately on farmers as a class, not just on those in difficulty.

Besides, this strategy would violate each of the lessons we drew from the Chrysler experience (Chapter 2). It would be a permanent bailout. It would offer no incentive for restored independence. And it would offer no opportunity for public participation in the benefits.

2. Change the Terms of Credit

The second basic strategy is to address the threat of insolvency by restructuring debt—forgiving some portion of the principal, reducing interest rates, or lengthening repayment periods. Most of the specific plans put forward in the past year have been variants of this strategy. One of them has actually been made official policy.

On September 18, 1984, President Reagan announced a plan to modify existing FmHA loan programs. There were two key points. The FmHA was allowed to defer, without interest, repayment of up to 25 percent of a qualified FmHA borrower's loan. Further, the FmHA was authorized to issue guarantees on troubled loans made by commercial banks and Farm Credit System lenders in return for a write-down of principal (at least 10 percent) adequate to produce a positive cash-flow for the debtor.

The first provision proved reasonably popular, as several thousand FmHA borrowers availed themselves of the deferral opportunity. The second, however, was far less successful. Private lenders refused to participate on the ground that a write-down of even 10 percent on their portfolio of troubled loans would dangerously erode their capital base, perhaps even push them below the minimum required by the Federal Reserve Board. In short, they argued that the administration's plan did not strike an acceptable balance between the interests of borrowers and creditors.

Pressure for change intensified through the fall and early winter. On February 6, 1985, the administration responded. New regulations allowed banks to qualify for loan guarantees by reducing either principal or interest rates.

It remains to be seen whether this liberalization of government policy will suffice to induce participation by private lending institutions. The Independent Bankers Association of America, representing primarily smaller and rural banks, argues that the federal government should help subsidize the lower interest rates offered by lending institutions as elements of restructured loans. A recently released report by the Office of Technology Assessment indicates that such subsidies would significantly increase the effectiveness of efforts to relieve distress and restore the viability of potentially profitable farms.

Prof. Neil Harl of Iowa State University has analyzed the costs of various burden-sharing proposals. Assuming an average interest write-down of 4.5 percent with the government providing 2 percent and participation rates ranging from 50 to 70 percent, depending on the debt-to-equity ratios of borrowers, subsidy costs to the federal government would be about $1.7 billion annually. With a participation rate of 100 percent, this figure would rise to $2.3 billion. In addition, to the extent that the government guarantees principal, additional taxpayer funds would be at risk, with ultimate costs determined by default rates and the percentage of loan obligations recoverable through the sale of collateral.

Many farm advocates at the state level have argued that debt restructuring will fail unless it is bolstered by temporary moratoria on farm foreclosures. It is alleged that good, credit-worthy farmers will be driven off their land before plans that are sound in the long run have had a chance to take hold. Lenders reply that they are making every effort to refrain from foreclosing and that a general moratorium would protect, not the farmers who need a breathing space, but rather those who cannot possibly recover. This, they conclude, would further weaken rural banks and reduce the availability of new credit, impeding or even freezing the process of adjustment. Although some state legislatures have seriously considered moratoria, such proposals have gained only limited support in the Congress.

3. Stabilize Land Values

A third strategy for dealing with the farm credit crisis involves public participation in the market for agricultural land. Advocates of this approach begin with the assumption that the value of land has fallen to levels roughly equal to its real economic worth (that is, the capitalized value of the income it can produce under current and projected conditions). Yet land prices continue to fall because forced sales are creating a glut on the market. This downward spiral is creating intense pressure on basically sound farmers and lending institutions. The solution, some argue, is a temporary intervention in the market to stabilize land prices at reasonable levels.

Proposals to implement this strategy have been advanced by Prof. Harl, the Farm Credit Council, and the American Farmland Trust. The details differ, but the underlying idea is that a newly created corporation would be authorized to acquire farmland at "fair market value" from creditors who would otherwise be compelled to foreclose. Rather than being thrown off the land, farmers would rent it from the corporation with opportunities and incentives to repurchase it if conditions improve. The difference between that rental income and the interest costs associated with the land would be a public subsidy. (Alternatively, the public subsidy could take the form of a direct cash payment of principal from the corporation to the creditor.) Funds needed for the operation of the corporation could be obtained through some combination of federal, state, and private investments. To the extent that land values not only stabilize but actually rise during the life of the corporation, some or all of the initial subsidy might be recovered upon resale of the land. On the other hand, to the extent that the land held by the corporation acts as a reserve overhanging the market, increases in land values would be restricted by the prospect of releasing the corporation's holdings into the market.

These proposals appear to meet many of the criteria derived from the Chrysler experience. They offer a temporary, not permanent, bailout; hold out hope that beneficiaries can regain their independence; and provide the public with a chance to participate directly in potential benefits. But the overall appropriateness of these proposals rests on the validity of the factual premises underlying them. While avoiding unnecessary forced liquidations and a financial panic is an important objective, no valid public purpose is served by artificially holding land prices above their real economic value. Arguments that prices have already declined to this point must therefore be rigorously examined.

SELECTED REFERENCES

Comptroller of the Currency, *Condition of the Agricultural Sector and Agricultural Banks*, February 1985.

Economic Research Service, USDA, "Financial Conditions of Farmers and Farm Lenders, 1984: A Background Paper Prepared for the Roosevelt Center's Roundtable Conference," November 1984.

John C. Obert and William A. Galston, *Down . . . Down . . . Down . . . On The Farm*. Roosevelt Center, April 1985.

Luther Tweeten, "Farm Financial Stress, Structure of Agriculture and Public Policy." American Enterprise Institute, January 1985.

Section III

Approaches To The Farm Bill

The purpose of Section III is to present and evaluate some of the most important options for dealing with the longer-term problems facing American agriculture. Each of these options is cast in the form of a proposed 1985 farm bill covering the four years 1986 to 1989.

Chapter 6 looks at the consequences of continuing current policies.

Chapter 7 explores the implications of dismantling existing government programs and subjecting agriculture to the free market.

Chapter 8 investigates the other extreme—an approach that seeks to resolve the perennial imbalance between agricultural supply and demand through a regime of strict government controls on production.

Chapter 9 examines the strategy of "mixed reform"—a collection of more narrowly focused programs, each designed to further a specific goal, the totality of which would aim for improved balance and consistency among the various elements of agricultural policy.

Finally, Chapter 10 compares the different effects of these four farm bill options on key economic and social indicators, on the central objectives of agricultural policy, and on the major groups that have intense and frequently conflicting interests in the outcome of this debate.

Each option includes programs for food grains (wheat and rice), feed grains (corn, sorghum, barley, oats, and rye), soybeans, and cotton. The other government programs (for dairy, peanuts, sugar, and tobacco) are not specifically treated. Readers interested in these commodities and their programs may consult Appendix A.

The quantitative evaluation of the predicted effects of the various options rests on a rigorous, multi-step estimation procedure. Readers interested in the details of this procedure may consult Appendix B.

Although farm programs are carefully specified through legislation, their operation requires a significant amount of administrative discretion. Readers interested in a detailed description of this discretion and a case-history of its effects may consult Appendix C.

Chapter 6

Continuation of Current Policy

Introduction

Agricultural policy is very slow to change. Most politicians find themselves squeezed between the farm lobby and budgetary constraints. They tend to make at most incremental changes in farm programs, usually in response to constituent pressures or economic distress. They have little incentive to advocate bold new approaches, and periodic crises evoke hastily devised nostrums rather than long-range solutions.

In spite of numerous criticisms of current policy, these factors suggest that continuing the collection of known, familiar programs already in place may well be the most politically palatable option in 1985. Proponents contend that the New Deal goal of enhancing farm incomes is still valid. They maintain that with improved administration, current programs can provide important economic assistance to beleaguered farmers at an acceptable cost. And they argue that the present rural crisis is no time to pull the rug out from under America's farmers.

Because current policy will be the point of departure for legislative debates and will provide the standard against which all competing proposals are measured, our examination of basic options begins here. This chapter examines how American agriculture is likely to perform if current policy is continued for four more years and assesses that projected performance in light of the goals previously discussed.

The Assumed Setting

To assess the performance of the farm sector over the four years (1986-1989) governed by the 1985 farm bill, we must specify both the expected economic environment for public policy and the details of that policy. We begin by describing our broad economic assumptions, which we will use as the background for considering each of the four policy options analyzed in this and subsequent chapters.

59

The Macroeconomic Setting

We assume moderate to strong economic growth in the domestic economy and moderate growth in the world economy. Domestic inflation remains low, and the budget deficit is slowly pared over several years, resulting in falling interest rates and gradual declines in the value of the dollar. This results in demand that grows in the rest of the world, albeit more slowly than in the 1970s. The domestic market continues its slow growth at a rate just slightly faster than population growth (about one percent per year).

Weather

The commodity programs, especially their costs, are significantly influenced by the weather both here and abroad. In large part, weather determines annual output and consequently short-run commodity supplies and their prices. Any analysis projecting the operation and performance of programs must therefore make some assumption about weather patterns. But it is impossible to predict future weather patterns in specific years or even across several years. This problem must be resolved somewhat arbitrarily. The accepted analytical convention, which we follow here, is to assume favorable weather. That assumption is reflected in our analysis by steady increases in crop yields per acre, at rates consistent with historical trends.

The weather, of course, is not constant from year to year. These real-life fluctuations cause commodity output to vary, with consequent variations in prices. Over the past 16 years, the annual U.S. grain output has varied from 31 percent below trend to 15 percent above trend. Prices have exhibited year-to-year changes ranging from an increase of 58 percent from the previous year to a decline of 17 percent.

For technical reasons rooted in the structure of commodity programs, steady rises in production in line with historical trends tend to increase the costs of these programs. Although we have assumed such steady rises, the probability of four consecutive years of stable domestic and global weather is virtually zero. Thus, in the 1986-89 period, it is quite likely that unpredictable weather deviations will cause significant departures from trends in both production and consumption. In that event, the costs of the programs to the Treasury would be less than estimates provided in this and following chapters. In our judgment, however, this is unlikely to have a significant effect on comparisons among the options.

Agricultural Productivity

Since World War II, productivity increases have been both strong and constant, even when markets and prices were relatively stagnant. We expect this trend to continue.

60

Mechanization, irrigation, fertilizer use, and improved management techniques have been largely responsible for past increases in productivity, but these technologies are now widely disseminated and well understood. Thus, future increases from these sources are likely to come at slower rates. Both public and private investments in productivity continue to be massive, however. Conservation tillage, more efficient irrigation and fertilization, and integrated pest management hold promise for short-term increases in efficiency. Biological innovations, including new hybrids, new techniques of genetic modification, and the use of hormones or stimulants, could have unprecedented impacts on yields and output. On balance, under the economic conditions assumed through 1989/90, yield increases would be expected to continue at current rates of about 1 percent annually.

Foreign and Domestic Demand

We assume that the current competitive tensions in world export markets continue at about the current level. That implies that the EEC continues its agricultural export subsidies and that exports continue to grow, although at a much slower rate than in the 1970s. In spite of concerns about the EEC policy, the United States does not adopt a regular policy of subsidized exports. No major shifts are assumed in the policies of other major trading nations.

To examine the outlook for U.S. exports, we analyzed trends in income and population growth, agricultural production, and food and agricultural policies for each important nation and region. Based on these estimates, we projected import demand and competition with U.S. exports for the balance of the 1980s.

A similar procedure was used to estimate changes in domestic use for each of the basic commodities, both for direct food use and for intermediate use as animal feeds and industrial raw materials. Income and population were the major determinants, together with trends in food preferences.

These assumptions imply that all other things being equal, U.S. exports will grow at rates about one-half those of the 1970s while the domestic market grows at about the same rate. By 1989, the volume of exports will be up about 17 percent from current levels. Continued productivity gains suggest that supply will tend to outpace demand, implying potential overabundance and surpluses.

Table 1.
Exports

Year	:	Corn	:	Wheat	:	Rice	:	Cotton	:	Soybeans	:	TOTAL
	:		mil bu		:	mil cwt	:	mil bales	:	mil bu	:	mil tons
1985/86	:	2,043		1,540		65.0		6.6		775		128.0
1986/87	:	2,075		1,600		67.0		6.7		810		131.7
1987/88	:	2,100		1,650		69.0		6.8		890		136.3
1988/89	:	2,150		1,750		72.0		7.2		975		143.3
1989/90	:	2,200		1,850		75.0		7.5		1,050		150.0

Current Programs

Commodity Programs

The major program tools for domestic crops are the price support loan program, direct payments, land set-aside and diversion, and the farmer-owned grain reserves. Mandatory supply controls and import restrictions have disappeared for the major crops, although they still are used for a few commodities including tobacco, sugar, peanuts, and dairy products.

In this chapter, as well as in the subsequent discussion of alternatives to current policy, we will deal with the major crops: food grains (wheat and rice), feed grains (corn, sorghum, barley, oats, and rye), soybeans, and cotton. These crops amount to nearly one-third of the total agricultural sector (Table 2). Livestock, which constitutes over one-half of the sector, has never been covered by commodity programs. Programs for other commodities raise complex and distinctive problems that cannot be fully dealt with in this study. (Readers interested in dairy, peanuts, sugar, and tobacco may consult Appendix A for descriptions of current programs in those areas.)

Table 2.
Farm Sector Cash Receipts, 1983

Item	Million $	Percent of Total
Livestock		
Cattle and Calves	28,694	
All Other Livestock	21,700	
Dairy Products	18,808	
TOTAL............................	69,202	46.3
Crops		
Grains, Oilseeds, & Cotton...................	42,140	
Hay	2,207	
Tobacco	2,831	
Vegetables & Melons.......................	8,233	
Fruits & Nuts	6,153	
All Other.................................	7,953	
TOTAL............................	69,517	46.5
Other Cash Receipts*...........................	1,539	1.0
Government Payments	9,294	6.2
Total Cash Receipts	149,552	100.0

*Machine hire, custom work, and recreational income.
Source: *Economic Indicators of the Farm Sector*, USDA.

Programs for grains include:

- *The nonrecourse loan program (popularly referred to as price supports).* Farmers place grain under loan for less than one year. The "loan rate" is the amount lent per unit of the commodity. If the price rises sufficiently to cover interest costs, the loan is likely to be repaid and the grain redeemed for sale in the market. If it is not redeemed, the CCC takes title to the grain. Hence, the CCC is a market of last resort, offering a guaranteed price.
- *Target price deficiency payments.* A target price is established for each commodity. If the market price fails to reach this target, the difference between the target and market prices (or between the target and the loan rate) is paid directly from the Treasury to the farmer.
- *Production control programs.* Farmers may be required to set aside cropland to become eligible for loan and deficiency payment programs. They may also be eligible for a direct payment for extra land diverted, if such a program is in effect.
- *The farmer-owned grain reserve.* This is essentially an extension of the loan program. Farmers agree to store grain for an extended period

or until market prices reach a specified level. In return, farmers receive a nonrecourse loan, storage payments, and some waiver of the interest on the loan.

- *Federal crop insurance.* This insurance provides protection against natural hazards. Farmers' premiums cover a part of the cost; the rest is a federal subsidy.

Although the upland cotton program is similar to those for grains, it gives market pricing somewhat greater weight. The loan rate is determined by a formula based on past prices in the U.S. and foreign markets, and deficiency payments are based upon the average market price for the calendar year. A special quota allows importation of additional cotton when domestic supplies are short.

The soybean program is the most market oriented of the commodity programs. There are no provisions for supply control or deficiency payments, and soybeans are specifically excluded from the commodity reserve. Nonrecourse loans are available, and the rate is set at 75 percent of the average market price in the previous five years, excluding the highest and lowest values.

Exports

Since the early 1970s, U.S. agricultural policy has depended in large part on world market growth to match increases in farm productivity and generate acceptable incomes to farmers. Beyond general efforts to enhance U.S. competitiveness and market share, there are two targeted export promotion programs: PL 480 (for concessional food exports and donations); and commercial export credit, primarily government guarantees for private commercial loans made to foreign purchasers of U.S. commodities.

PL 480 serves several objectives: surplus disposal, economic development, emergency food assistance, foreign policy, and market development. Surplus disposal has a lower priority today than in the past.

The commercial credit program guarantees private bank loans made at commercial rates and involves no subsidy other than the federal guarantee. Commercial loans also are made directly by the CCC, frequently at concessional interest rates. The two may be combined to provide "blended" credit, with the total loan package consisting of up to 20 percent of the loan at zero interest and the balance at commercial rates. The Department of Agriculture also has authority to provide intermediate term credit to finance investments that will promote market development, but this program has been virtually unused.

Since the 1981 Act, the precipitous decline in agricultural exports has made export expansion a major concern. Congress has provided authority for greater direct export credit and CCC credit guarantees, and it has increased funding for PL 480 (particularly long-term credit sales). In fiscal 1984, the budget for PL 480 sales was over $1.5 billion ($872 million in concessional sales). Four billion dollars in export credit guarantees and $175 million in direct export credit were also made available.

Resource Conservation

The Department of Agriculture operates several conservation and pollution abatement programs, including technical assistance to landowners and local governments, cost sharing for conservation practices through the Great Plains Conservation Program, surveys and forecasts of the nation's soil and water resources, and programs to address long-term needs in soil and water conservation. In addition, USDA operates programs to preserve wetlands and provide assistance for emergency conservation measures, nonindustrial forest development, and improved water management in the Colorado River basin.

The 1981 farm bill authorized several new conservation programs, including technical and financial assistance for areas with serious resource problems, grants to local governments for conservation expenses, and conservation loans for producers. However, no funds have been provided for any of these programs.

Credit, Rural Development, and Family Farms

The Department of Agriculture subsidizes credit to farmers through the Farmers Home Administration (FmHA) as well as through the CCC. Through the farm ownership and operating loan programs, FmHA acts as a "lender of last resort" to farmers unable to obtain credit from other sources. Farmers suffering from natural disaster or economic distress are eligible for emergency disaster or economic emergency loans.

FmHA provides credit to support rural development through loans and grants for rural housing, community facilities, water and waste disposal systems, and for rural businesses and industries. The Rural Electrification Administration (REA) also supports rural development by providing federally subsidized loans and guarantees for projects to expand electric and telephone services in rural areas.

Current Policy Extended

Extending current programs would require adapting them to the economic environment of the late 1980s—in particular, record budget deficits and increased international competition. The following program descriptions rest on what we believe to be reasonable assumptions as to what this process of adaptation would entail.

Commodity Loans

In recent years, loan rates have been kept below market prices, enhancing the ability of our commodities to compete abroad. But recent world prices have been low enough to reawaken concern that the loans are impeding U.S. access to world markets.

Some farm groups would prefer higher loan rates, while other groups and the Administration would prefer to see them lower. In examining current policy over 1986/87 - 1989/90, we assume that loan rates remain at levels set for 1984/85, except for those commodities for which the loan rate is set by market price formulas (cotton and soybeans) (Table 3).

Table 3.
Loan Rates

Commodity	1980/81	1981/82	1982/83	1983/84	1984/85	1986/87 to 1989/90
Corn	2.25	2.40	2.55	2.65	2.55	2.55
Sorghum	2.14	2.28	2.42	2.52	2.42	2.42
Wheat	3.00	3.20	3.55	3.65	3.30	3.30
Rice	7.12	8.01	8.14	8.14	8.00	8.00
Cotton	48.00	52.50	57.10	55.00	55.00	56.57
Soybeans	5.02	5.02	5.02	5.02	5.02	5.11

NOTE: Prices are dollars per bushel except rice (dollars per cwt) and cotton (cents per pound).

Target Price Deficiency Payments

We assume that the deficiency payments programs will continue, with target prices frozen at the levels of 1984 and the payment limitation per farm held at $50,000 (Table 4).

Table 4.
Target Prices

Year	Wheat	Corn	Rice	Cotton
	$/bu	$/bu	$/cwt	$/lb
1982	4.05	2.70	10.85	0.17
1983	4.30	2.86	11.40	0.76
1984*	4.38	3.03	11.90	0.81
1985*	4.38	3.03	11.90	0.81
1986	4.38	3.03	11.90	0.81

* As modified by the Agricultural Programs Adjustment Act of 1984.

Production Control

We assume that authority for supply control programs is continued, both for the voluntary set-aside programs and for paid diversion. Because paid diversion programs are more popular than the voluntary set-asides and current law requires that both programs be used together, we assume that when the voluntary cuts are used, paid diversion programs also will be offered, using the flat-rate system, under which producers who set aside cropland are eligible to receive an amount per acre based on the yield history of the diverted land.

Farmer-Owned Reserve (FOR)

In the past, special higher loan rates were available for grain entering the FOR, and these loans were sometimes interest free. Since 1981, FOR loan rates have been the same as regular loans, and interest is charged as soon as the grain enters the reserve. We assume that the FOR is continued with only minor modifications.

Export Promotion

The continuation of curent policy assumes no basic change in export promotion and market development strategies. We assume that both PL 480 and the commercial credit programs grow relatively slowly. While PL 480 may distribute surpluses somewhat more actively, it would continue to be focused on the world's poorest countries and to be constrained by the need to avoid interfering with commercial markets. The commercial credit programs will continue to face limits on the amount of authorized subsidies.

Resource Conservation

The extension of current policy assumes no major change in ongoing programs. The annual budget of about $1 billion would be used largely for technical assistance for individual farmers, with relatively small amounts for conservation cost-sharing and watershed development. Under this scenario, no major efforts are made to unify conservation and commodity policy, and no new conservation efforts are required as a condition of eligibility for commodity program benefits.

Performance of Agriculture under Extension of Current Programs

Overall Picture

Within our assumed economic framework, the continuation of current policy would leave the farm sector in its current recession well into the next four-year cycle. Only in the final two years would the economic performance of agriculture begin to improve.

This situation would be quite reminiscent of the 1960s: large, moderately growing export and domestic markets overshadowed by excess production. Market prices would be too low to eliminate pressure on producers, but government price protections would be too large to permit really significant economic adjustment. Output would continue to grow faster than use until at least the third year.

Interest rates and capital costs would continue to exert significant pressure, but more selectively than the inflation-fed cost/price squeeze of the late 1970s. Farmers with the highest ratios of debt to assets would be hard hit, while those with lower ratios would be relatively unscathed.

During the third and fourth years, world markets would strengthen. Markets for U.S. products would expand. Commodity use would come into closer balance with production, allowing slightly declining stocks and stronger prices.

Production

In spite of the distressed state of the farm economy, government programs would preclude significant adjustment, and production would continue to

68

grow. In the four years, aggregate output would rise over four percent, outpacing domestic and foreign use in the first two years.

Table 5.
Continuation of Current Policy:
Program Crop Acreage and Production

Item	1980	1981	1982	1983	1984	1985	1986	1987	1988	1989
	— — — million acres — — —									
Area										
Planted	292.5	300.0	295.7	248.3	284.5	280.3	278.8	280.1	276.7	281.7
Area Idled	0	0	10.7	75.6	29.9	25.9	26.1	27.6	30.7	29.7
TOTAL (Base										
Acreage)	292.5	300.0	306.4	323.9	314.4	306.2	304.9	307.7	307.4	311.4
% Idled	0	0	3.5	23.3	9.5	8.5	8.6	9.0	10.0	9.5
	— — — million tons — — —									
Production	321.1	388.3	395.2	253.3	364.5	370.6	375.7	382.3	383.0	391.6
	— — — tons — — —									
Production/ Acre	1.10	1.29	1.34	1.02	1.28	1.32	1.35	1.36	1.38	1.39

This growth in production would occur in spite of extensive government attempts to control production. An average of 28.5 million acres (more than nine percent of the program crop acreage base) would be idled over the four years. Only in the final year of the period would conditions improve enough to allow any reduction in idled acreage.

Domestic and Export Use

By the first year of the new farm bill, domestic use would have recovered from the recession and the shock of PIK and returned to the trend growth path of just over one percent annually (Table 6). Export growth would average 3.5 percent annually over the four years. The combination of domestic and export use would provide a steady growth of about two percent annually in total use.

69

Table 6.
Continuation of Current Policy:
Program Crop Domestic and Export Use

Item	1980	1981	1982	1983	1984	1985	1986	1987	1988	1989
				— — — million tons — — —						
Domestic Use	203.0	212.6	229.2	208.9	218.6	233.7	237.0	243.4	246.5	246.8
Export	135.9	137.2	124.0	118.9	132.5	128.0	131.7	136.3	143.3	150.0
TOTAL USE	338.9	349.8	353.2	327.8	351.1	361.7	368.7	379.7	389.8	396.8
Export Value* (billion dollars)						18.9	19.4	20.1	22.2	23.3

* Valued at the farm level price.

Stocks

Despite the idling of almost 10 percent of all cropland, stocks would grow by 7 million metric tons (mmt) at the end of the current marketing year and by another 3 mmt in the following year. Only in 1988 would the combination of acreage control and stronger export growth reduce large stocks.

Table 7.
Continuation of Current Policy:
Ending Year Commodity Stocks

Commodity	1980	1981	1982	1983	1984	1985	1986	1987	1988	1989
					— — — million tons — — —					
Grains	62.4	102.0	142.0	73.9	85.6	95.0	101.5	103.4	99.0	93.0
Soybeans	8.5	6.9	9.4	4.8	6.8	8.5	8.9	9.6	7.4	8.4
Cotton	0.6	1.5	1.7	0.7	1.0	1.0	1.1	1.1	1.0	0.8
TOTAL	71.5	110.4	153.1	79.4	93.4	104.5	111.5	114.1	107.4	102.2
Reserve	14.7	55.2	76.4	31.9	35.2	40.2	47.2	48.5	45.9	42.1
CCC	13.5	15.6	40.5	13.8	19.6	22.3	23.5	23.5	23.6	23.6
Free	43.3	39.6	36.2	33.7	38.6	42.0	40.8	42.1	37.9	36.5
TOTAL	71.5	110.4	153.1	79.4	93.4	104.5	111.5	114.1	107.4	102.2
As % of Domestic & Export Use			43.3	24.2	26.6	28.9	30.2	30.0	27.5	25.7

Heading into the 1986 crop year, the FOR would contain a significant proportion of the total grain stocks and remain essentially full over the entire period. Prices would never rise enough to trigger the reserves.

Commodity Prices

There would be little opportunity for any appreciable strength in commodity prices over the life of the legislation. In fact, prices would remain under considerable pressure in the first two years as stocks continue to accumulate (Table 8). However, prices for most commodities would firm up in the last two years as use grows and stocks are slightly reduced.

Table 8.
Continuation of Current Policy:
Program Commodity Prices

Commodity	1980	1981	1982	1983	1984	1985	1986	1987	1988	1989
Corn	3.11	2.50	2.68	3.20	2.68	2.67	2.72	2.71	2.72	2.75
Sorghum	2.94	2.39	2.52	2.75	2.45	2.42	2.40	2.42	2.50	2.55
Barley	2.86	2.45	2.23	2.50	2.35	2.38	2.35	2.32	2.31	2.32
Rye	2.63	2.99	2.41	2.40	2.10	2.30	2.35	2.37	2.40	2.38
Oats	1.79	1.89	1.48	1.69	1.72	1.74	1.72	1.68	1.60	1.50
Wheat	3.91	3.65	3.55	3.54	3.42	3.45	3.43	3.41	3.45	3.48
Rice	12.80	9.05	8.11	8.79	8.30	8.20	8.15	8.20	8.45	9.00
Soybeans	7.57	6.04	5.69	7.75	6.20	6.00	5.92	5.80	6.50	6.30
Cotton	74.7	54.3	59.4	66.4	65.0	67.0	65.0	65.0	68.0	70.0

NOTE: Prices are dollars per bushel except rice (dollars per cwt) and cotton (cents per pound).

Farm Income

Receipts from the sale of farm products would increase slightly across the period, primarily reflecting growth in output. The largest increase would occur in the fourth year, when receipts reflect the slight strengthening of prices as well as the increase in output. Production expenses for crop farmers would grow in proportion to volume growth, maintaining a stable relationship between receipts and costs.

This scenario would be advantageous for the livestock sector. Abundant feed supplies and relatively stable prices could be expected to produce growing receipts and incomes for livestock farmers.

While both cash receipts and production expenses for the sector would continue to grow, net farm income would not increase. From 1980 through 1985 (forecast), farm income averaged about $25 billion, with swings from $16 to $31 billion. Farm income would average $24.6 billion annually in 1986-1989, essentially unchanged from the previous level, and slightly lower once inflation is taken into account.

Table 9.
Continuation of Current Policy:
Value of Program Commodity Sales/Net Farm Income

Item	1980	1981	1982	1983	1984	1985	1986	1987	1988	1989
				— — — billion dollars — — —						
Value of Sales	55.6	47.4	50.5	48.2	50.0	49.9	51.8	53.4	55.3	56.9
Net Farm Income	21.3	31.0	22.3	16.1	31.0	22.5	23.6	24.3	25.1	25.3

Program Costs

Continuation of current policy is not an inexpensive option. Even with target prices frozen, continued growth in output would cause direct payments to rise considerably. The deficiency payment program, FOR storage, and land diversion payments are expected to total $16.9 billion under the 1981 Act (with current projections of 1985 payments), an average of $4.2 billion each year. For 1986-1989, those payments could reach $21.5 billion, an annual average of $5.4 billion (Table 10).

Table 10.
Continuation of Current Policy:
Program Cost Summary

Item	:	1985	:	1986	:	1987	:	1988	:	1989
				— — — million dollars — — —						
Deficiency Payments		3,998.0		3,849.4		3,932.5		3,620.8		3,403.2
Storage		410.0		483.0		496.0		470.0		430.0
Land Diversion		742.0		1,092.0		1,113.0		1,285.0		1,300.0
TOTAL		5,150.0		5,424.4		5,541.5		5,375.8		5,133.2

Deficiency payments would be the largest costs, averaging $3.7 billion annually, about 70 percent of which would go to producers of the two major crops, corn and wheat. With the FOR remaining large, storage payments to farmers would average $463 million annually. Attempts to control production through paid land diversion would average $1.2 billion annually.

These figures reflect only the direct payments programs for the major crops. Total program costs include the CCC price support loan costs, which could be considerable. For example, both corn and wheat prices would av-

73

erage very close to the respective loan rates, suggesting that forfeitures could be large in some years. Additionally, CCC net interest expenses (the difference between costs of its borrowings from the Treasury and receipts from its relending) could amount to $1.5 billion or more annually. And costs for the dairy and minor commodity programs could approach $2 billion annually.

Food Prices

Food prices would be little affected by a continuation of current policy. Any overall rise in food prices would primarily reflect processing and other costs beyond the farm. And those increases would not be expected to exceed the overall rate of inflation. Barring protracted bad weather, consumers would face virtually no pressure from food price increases.

Evaluation

Overall Performance

This "current policy" approach yields results little changed from those of the past four years. Its strengths are the relatively stable flow of cash receipts and government payments it provides to an industry under significant economic pressure and the protection against crop failures that its large stocks offer consumers. But that stability comes at a significant cost, because it retards industry adjustment to current world and domestic markets. For example, the wheat price averages a relatively low $3.40 to $3.50, signalling overabundance and need to reduce production. But the $4.38 target price induces continued surplus output and taxpayer support of farm incomes.

At the same time, production control efforts are increasingly ineffective. Target prices have to be maintained to attract farmer participation in voluntary acreage reduction programs, in essence using higher prices in an attempt to bring about less production. The effect is predictable, with the higher prices only serving to stimulate production. Price support programs encourage nonparticipating farmers to expand their production and thus offset reductions from participants. Even participating farmers may not reduce production much because they can idle their least productive acres first and then apply more fertilizer to their remaining land. In addition, administration of the programs allows a substantial amount of "slippage," so that the actual acreage reduction often is much less than the officially determined acreage reduction.

74

Food Safety, Quality, and Prices

The continuation of current policy would be unlikely to produce any perceptible change in the quality and safety of the food supply. It could be viewed, as could most other policy approaches, as essentially neutral with respect to this goal.

This policy approach also is unlikely to produce any important changes in the recent levels or patterns of food prices. But it fails to address the inherent contradiction among government programs, some of which work to reduce prices while others have the effect of raising them, with both efforts entailing large taxpayer costs. Also, current programs clearly hold prices for some commodities higher than they otherwise would be and at considerable cost to consumers (several billions of dollars for dairy products and sugar alone).

Resource Conservation

Current policy does not fare well when evaluated against the objective of resource conservation. The effectiveness of programs that explicitly address soil erosion and water quality problems is questionable, and the contradiction between these programs and those that encourage production is severe. Moreover, current policy fails to change incentives in ways that would be more conducive to wiser resource use and management. Thus, continuing current policy does nothing to address the fundamental problems, let alone clarify the overall direction of resource use and conservation policy.

Farm Income and Structure

1. Farm Income

The continuation of current policy would do nothing to improve farm income over its levels of recent years. This level of farm income would be unlikely to reverse the current negative rates of return on investment. This implies further deflation of asset values (primarily land), continuing until they reach levels at which the income they produce yields a return comparable to returns on investments available elsewhere in the economy.

2. Farm Structure

It is difficult to assess the impact of current farm programs on farm structure. Some experts believe that loan and target-price programs aid family-size farms while paid diversion helps larger operators. The programs may keep some farmers who would otherwise fail in business, but they may also place larger farms in a position to acquire other farms and further increase the concentration of production. Overall, the continuation of current programs would do little to resist or reverse trends that, in the aggregate, are working against the survival of family-size farms.

Economic Growth and Competitiveness

1. Stability

Continuation of current policy gets mixed marks at best when evaluated relative to the goal of stability. First, recent experience suggests that it would not preclude boom-bust cycles. Indeed, current policy is widely held to have exacerbated rather than dampened the swings of the past decade. At the same time, it is clear that current policy does provide some diminution of shorter-term instability. But that stability comes at a high price, in steadily increasing direct Treasury outlays and in the continuing misallocation of resources.

2. Exports

We are now in the fourth year of falling exports, with forecasts that provide little basis for optimism. But continuation of current policy would do little to resolve the conflict between export expansion and the export-retarding effects of high price supports and production controls. (This contradiction is exacerbated by the increasing use of commodity programs to soften the export-dampening consequences of macroeconomic policy.) Over time, current policies lead to a generally acrimonious trade environment with sporadic trade actions, threats of retaliatory measures, and a rising trend of protectionism.

A critical determinant of the future performance of U.S. agriculture is the responsiveness of foreign buyers to the price of our products, both in the short run and the long run. When prices rise, how much less will be purchased? When prices fall, how much will sales increase?

This ratio is known as the "elasticity of demand." Determining its value is a highly controversial issue within the agricultural industry and among economists. It is, however, much more than a technical argument. It is fundamental to how agriculture might fare under different proposed policy approaches, and thus to the evaluation of those approaches.

In particular, how much lower will exports be if we maintain current price supports for commodities? Conversely, if the United States were to lower supports to world market levels, would our sales expand sufficiently to offset the lower price that we would receive for each unit sold? Will exports expand enough to increase farm income? If so, how long would this take?

An example will illustrate the problem. In 1984, wheat exports were 1,600 million bushels. The price for the marketing season averaged $3.50 per bushel, producing total export revenues of $5.6 billion. Many analysts argue that we could have sold more had the loan rate of $3.30 not prevented prices from heading lower. Would it have been worthwhile?

Estimates of *short-run* demand elasticity for wheat vary from –0.16 to –0.8. (That is, for every 1 percent decline in price, demand would rise between 0.16 and 0.8 percent.) If it were –0.16 and the price dropped 10 percent to $3.15, exports would increase 1.6 percent, or 25.6 million bushels, generating revenues of $5.121 billion. At –0.8, a 10 percent price decline would increase exports 8 percent to 1,728 million bushels, generating revenues of $5.443 billion. This means that falling prices would result in declining total revenues, even though sales volume increases. In short, reducing government price supports would reduce revenues for farmers, even though exports increase.

But what about the longer run? If demand becomes more responsive to price changes over time, the revenue picture changes significantly. Most analysts agree that long-run elasticity rises significantly, but they disagree about the extent and timing of the increase.

If long-run elasticity were 1.5, then a 10 percent reduction in the price would generate a 15 percent expansion in exports, to 1,840 million bushels, which at $3.15 per bushel would generate revenues of $5.796 billion, an increase of $196 million over current levels.

Exports	Price	Revenues	Elasticity
(mil bu)	($/bu)	(bil $)	
1,600.0	3.50	5.600	
1,625.6	3.15	5.121	−0.16
1,728.0	3.15	5.443	−0.80
1,840.0	3.15	5.796	−1.50

Reviews of available studies lead us to the judgment that while the delineation between the short and long run is imprecise, demand does indeed become more elastic over time. However, the four-year period considered here is unlikely to be long enough for exports to respond fully to price declines. Thus, during the life of the 1985 farm bill, the maintenance of current policies would probably yield more income and revenue to farmers than would policy shifts toward free market prices. In the long run, the reverse may well be the case. But it is not difficult to understand why farmers who cannot long survive at current levels of income would resist long-term gains that are accompanied by short-term losses.

Foreign Responsibilities

Continuation of current policies would do little to clarify the goals or improve the effectiveness of our foreign agricultural programs. Because of the abundance, high stocks, and stable prices resulting from the continuation of current policy, emergency food aid could actually grow somewhat. But high production could well bring renewed emphasis on the use of PL 480 for surplus disposal, increasing disincentives for third world agricultural development and contradicting one of the key announced goals of U.S. policy.

SELECTED REFERENCES

Council for Agricultural Science and Technology, *The Emerging Economics of Agriculture: Review and Policy Options.* Report No. 98, Ames, Iowa, September 1983.

R.G. Chambers and R.E. Just, "Effects of Exchange Rate Changes on U.S. Agriculture: A Dynamic Analysis." *American Journal of Agricultural Economics*, 63:32-46, 1981.

John Dunmore and James Longmire, *Sources of Recent Changes in U.S. Agricultural Exports.* Economic Research Service, USDA, January 1984.

Jim Longmire and Art Morey, *Strong Dollar Dampens Demand for U.S. Farm Exports.* FAER 193, Economic Research Service, USDA, December 1983.

Greg McCune, Greg, "Farm Bill Outcome Linked to Elasticity Debate." Reuters News Service, February 20, 1985.

Chapter 7.

The Free Market

Introduction

The free-market approach calls for a greatly reduced role for government in the production and marketing of agricultural products, to be achieved by dismantling the commodity programs that directly influence farmers' decisions. While a market-oriented policy has long had a substantial number of adherents, support for it has been growing in recent years as the costs of existing programs have risen and their perceived effectiveness has declined. The Reagan Administration's 1985 farm legislation proposal is one variant of the free-market strategy.

Arguments for this approach are both positive, based on the alleged economic advantages of greater reliance on the market, and negative, citing the allegedly counterproductive effects of current programs.

The positive argument rests on standard propositions about the efficiency of markets. It is argued that if the resources devoted to food production were allocated in response to market signals, they would be devoted to those uses that would maximize their economic value. The result would be economic growth, higher GNP and per capita incomes, and improved standards of living. Moreover, proponents argue that in the long run, a freer market is in the best economic interests of farmers. Unshackled from restrictive programs, farmers will become even more efficient and more competitive in the world markets. Without the uncertainties and distortions of these programs, they will be able to organize their resources to respond more quickly and flexibly to the market.

Negative arguments for the free market approach rest on considerations of the cost, inefficiency, demand reduction, and inequity allegedly inherent in government intervention.

There is general agreement among analysts that the aggregate gains to farmers from the present programs are less than their costs to consumers and taxpayers. The difference is administrative expenses, efficiency losses from a product mix that does not allocate resources according to consumer demands, and the costs of idled land—all unproductive losses to society.

Proponents argue that in a dynamic market economy such as ours, continual adjustment is required. Certain segments of the economy may decline while others flourish. While there may be a role for government in helping ease the burdens of adjustment, it should not attempt to prevent adjustment. But, say the advocates of the market, this is precisely what the commodity programs do. They override or mask the market signals and delay (or even prevent) the needed adjustments. Taxpayers then are asked to support this inefficiency. For example, wheat farmers, responding to a guaranteed price of $4.38 per bushel rather than to a market price closer to $3.50, annually produce 200 million to 300 million bushels more than needed. The same is true for other grains, cotton, dairy, sugar, peanuts, and other commodities.

The artificial incentives hold resources in production long after relative market demands have shifted. While there are no reliable estimates of the overall costs of the resulting resource misallocations, they are large enough to significantly retard national economic growth.

The 1984 *Economic Report of the President* stated in this regard:

> Different rates of protection to different sectors tend to cause inefficient resource allocation. Resources tend to move to where they earn the highest returns. If public policy artificially raises the returns in one sector relative to another, this will attract excessive investment and result in excess capacity. Inefficient resource allocation lowers the potential production of the economy as a whole and reduces per capita income. When public policy diverts, say, investment capital or water from more to less productive use, this lowers national income.

In the long run, say free market advocates, these policies don't even help their intended beneficiaries, the farmers. Higher commodity prices are soon capitalized in rising land values, which increase the cost of production and debt burdens for new entrants into agriculture. Barriers may be raised so high that many innovative and energetic potential entrants are kept out completely.

While proponents of less government involvement point to these indirect costs, they also cite direct taxpayer costs. By the time the 1981 farm bill expires, agricultural programs will have cost taxpayers over $79 billion, an amount equivalent to 12 percent of the federal deficit in those years.

Federal programs are not only expensive, but—it is alleged—incoherent and contradictory. Taxpayer dollars support agricultural research and development and other programs that work to enhance productivity and lower food prices. But price supports, coupled with restrictive trade and marketing practices, artificially raise farm prices and offset these effects.

Proponents of the free market argue that the commodity programs inhibit agriculture from realizing its full export potential in two ways. First, politically determined support prices are frequently above world market prices, reducing the competitiveness of our products and diminishing export revenues in the long run. Second, price supports and production controls encourage our competitors, who are assured that our supplies will not be sold below our guaranteed floor prices. The long-term result is a lost share of world food markets. These effects mean not only lower export revenues and farm income, but also the loss of economic activity associated with an expanding export sector. For example, assuming stable prices, as many as 33,000 full-time jobs are generated by each $1 billion in additional agricultural export revenues. And to the extent that added foreign sales reflect the combination of lower prices and higher volume, job creation is even more significant. Thus, while agriculture already makes important contributions to the national economy through trade, it could do even more without interference from government programs.

Our trade posture is affected by the programs in other ways as well. The United States endorses free trade and works to that end in international negotiations, but that position is undermined by the restrictive trade practices that we must use to prevent imports from undermining our programs. In fact, we have argued for special exclusions from trade agreements to protect our dairy, sugar, and other commodities. It is extremely difficult to argue that others should lower their barriers and give us access to their markets when we are maintaining protective barriers of our own.

While free market advocates acknowledge that some greater instability may be inherent in their approach, they also argue that with the development of new institutions such as expanded options and futures markets, instability can be successfully managed by individual farmers. And they point out that one major source of instability—that stemming from government actions—would be greatly reduced. Actions such as announcing four different wheat programs in a matter of a few weeks, changing program rules regularly before almost every election, and lurching from little or no idled acreage to 20 percent of the cropland all create great uncertainty and exacerbate farmers' difficulties in making their production and investment decisions.

Finally, advocates of free market policies argue that current programs are inequitable, providing benefits only to farmers who happen to produce certain commodities and awarding disproportionate benefits to the largest farmers.

Varieties of Free Market Policies

There are several variants of this policy approach, distinguished by the pace at which the present programs are to be dismantled and by the extent of the residual role of government. Political support for a "cold turkey" approach—the abrupt termination of programs—is small, especially in the face of current distress in the farm economy. Most proponents would argue

81

that some transition is required to avoid severe capital losses and extreme difficulties for many. In the words of one, Don Paarlberg:

> It is enough to ask of the open market system that it handle satisfactorily the ongoing problems of supply and demand. It is too much to expect it also to correct, quickly and with minimal difficulties, the dislocations that result from 50 years of government intervention.

However, there appears to be little consensus about the length of an appropriate transition period.

There is considerable divergence of views about the extent of the government role in related areas such as grain reserves, conservation programs, the FmHA, and export promotion. However, most free market advocates agree in principle that research and education as well as inspection and grading services are legitimate functions of government (although for the latter, greater cost sharing through imposition of user fees is gaining favor).

The question of the role for government in export promotion is both philosophical and pragmatic. Recognizing the extent of the adjustment that is required, specifically the excess capacity that could exist in the short-run, there is considerable support for an even stronger role for government in this activity. It is argued that the transition can be eased by aggressively promoting exports to absorb more of the excess capacity and that this would be less expensive than continuing to make large deficiency payments and paying to idle excess acreage. Proponents of this approach also recognize the possibility that this course will provoke greater confrontation with our trading competitors but argue that it is necessary to counter their trading practices.

Description of the Free Market Program

The policy option specified and analyzed here would work toward a freer market by cutting back or phasing out the current programs over the next four years.

Price Supports

This approach embraces the premise that the price support loan program is no longer needed either to support prices or to ensure orderly markets. Thus, the loan program would be phased out and the CCC excluded from the banking business. During the transition, the loan rates for the major commodities would be based on a three-year moving average of the market price received by farmers and limited to 75 percent of that average. By the time the 1985 Act expires, they probably would be well below the world market price. The projected loan rates are shown in Table 1.

Table 1. Market Policy: Commodity Loan Rates

Commodity	:	1985	:	1986	:	1987	:	1988	:	1989
Corn		2.55		2.15		1.96		1.93		1.88
Sorghum		2.42		1.94		1.76		1.71		1.67
Barley		2.08		1.77		1.72		1.67		1.61
Oats		1.31		1.22		1.25		1.20		1.14
Wheat		3.30		2.60		2.52		2.48		2.43
Rice		8.00		6.29		6.24		5.99		4.87
Soybeans		5.02		5.00		4.54		4.28		4.20
Cotton		57.3		47.2		48.0		46.7		46.3

NOTE: Prices are dollars per bushel except rice (dollars per cwt) and cotton (cents per pound).

Income Supports

This approach would continue the target price/deficiency payments program for the major commodities but would successively lower the target price and reduce the payment limit for each farmer. Specifically, the target price would be a declining percentage of the three-year moving average of prices received by farmers, as follows:

Year	Percent
1986	100
1987	95
1988	90
1989	85

The projected target prices are shown in Table 2. The payment limit would be reduced from the current $50,000 per farmer to $20,000 in 1986, $15,000 in 1987, and $10,000 thereafter in order to target the programs to smaller farmers and reduce costs.

83

Table 2.
Market Policy: Commodity Target Prices

Commodity	:	1985	:	1986	:	1987	:	1988	:	1989
Corn		3.03		2.87		2.49		2.32		2.14
Sorghum		2.88		2.58		2.23		2.06		1.89
Barley		2.60		2.36		2.18		2.00		1.82
Oats		1.60		1.63		1.59		1.45		1.30
Wheat		4.38		3.50		2.91		2.97		2.76
Rice		11.90		8.37		7.90		7.19		6.65
Soybeans		—		—		—		—		—
Cotton		81.0		62.9		60.8		56.1		52.4

NOTE: Prices are dollars per bushel except rice (dollars per cwt) and cotton (cents per pound).

Production Control

Authority for production control would be continued and would rely on voluntary set-asides and diversion programs. When production control is required (as would be expected for at least the first three years of the program), a voluntary set-aside (with no direct payment for acres idled) would be imposed as a condition of eligibility for income supports, as follows:

Year	Set-Aside
1986	15%
1987	10%
1988	5%
1989	0%

Commodity Reserves

During the transition, we assume that a modified commodity reserve would continue for the crops now eligible. A single reserve would be established for wheat and feed grains, combining the disaster reserve, emergency feed reserve, all future loan forfeitures under CCC, and the international wheat reserve. Grain would enter the reserve at the regular loan rate, and remain until the release price is reached. No interest subsidy would be paid, and the current storage payment would remain. The reserve would be replenished only when stocks of either feed grains or wheat fall below 500 million bushels.

Resource Conservation

The present soil conservation programs would continue at current or reduced funding levels, but modified to target funds for technical and cost-sharing assistance. Farmers who till highly erosive land without an approved conservation plan would be ineligible for all federal farm program benefits for commodities grown on that land or any other land they work. There would be no long-term conservation reserve.

Export Promotion

While government's role is reduced in other aspects of this proposal, greater efforts to expand exports would be needed to do business in world markets where other countries regularly provide export subsidies.

Performance of Agriculture under the Free Market

Incorporated in the 1985 farm bill, this policy would mark the beginning of a rapid transition to much greater reliance on the market. It would also initiate a fundamental change in farmers' expectations, based on the clear signal that the commodity programs were being phased out and that appropriate adjustments must begin. Considerable anxiety would accompany it since, except for a brief period in the 1970s, we have had little experience with an agricultural economy in which the programs were not highly influential or even dominant. Substantial adjustments would undoubtedly be required, but it is difficult to project precisely what they will be and how they will occur.

This program would begin with the 1986 season, with the program provisions announced in advance. The likely performance of the agricultural sector in this transition period is described in this section.

Production

In making their operating decisions for the 1986 crops, producers would see lower production incentives from the programs, in the form of lower target prices, loan rates, and (for some farmers) payment limits. These changes would reduce the attractiveness of the programs. However, the existing economic pressure on many producers would encourage enrollment, and overall participation in the first years would be little different from recent experience.

Total plantings in 1986 would fall from 1985 levels by five and one-half million acres (Table 3). At the same time, 16 million acres would be enrolled in the voluntary set-aside. Adjustment would begin, and combined plantings plus acreage idled would be 291 million acres, 15 million acres less than the previous year, probably reflecting the phasing-out of the most marginally productive land that had remained in production only so long as the programs made it economically feasible. This contraction of the cropland base would be expected to continue as the program incentives decline in subsequent years. By 1989, the actual cropland base could be some 16 million acres (about five percent) less than when the program began.

Table 3.
Market Policy: Program Crop Acreage and Production

Item	:	1982	1983	1984	1985	1986	1987	1988	1989
					- - - million acres - - -				
Area Planted		295.7	248.3	284.5	280.3	274.8	281.4	283.6	290.1
Area Idled		10.7	75.6	29.9	25.9	16.2	9.6	4.2	0
TOTAL									
(Base Acreage)		306.4	323.9	314.4	306.2	291.0	291.0	287.8	290.1
% Idled		3.5	23.3	9.5	8.5	5.6	3.3	1.5	0
					- - - million tons - - -				
Production		395.2	253.3	364.5	370.6	368.6	386.1	396.2	408.5
					- - - tons - - -				
Production/Acre		1.34	1.02	1.28	1.32	1.34	1.37	1.40	1.41

The area actually planted increases by almost ten million acres over four years. Even so, it would be less than the area planted in 1982. Moreover, idled acreage is phased out completely by the last year of the program. Overall, the average annual plantings for the four years would be less than two percent below the average under the 1981 law (excepting the atypical year of PIK) while area idled by programs would be less than one-fifth the amount in 1982-85. The percentage of the base idled falls from an average of 11.2 in 1982-85 to 2.6 percent.

In 1986, production would be two million metric tons (mmt) below the previous year. Despite reduced program incentives, it expands every year thereafter, surpassing 400 mmt in 1989. Yields per acre would continue to rise.

Domestic and Export Use

The domestic consumption of program commodities would increase in the first year in response to lower prices (Table 4). Use would rise from 234 mmt in 1985 to 242 mmt in 1986 and continue to grow at a rate averaging

1.6 percent per year. Annual average use in 1989 would be eight percent higher than in 1985.

Export volume would grow at an average annual rate of 4 percent. The value of export sales would rise almost $4 billion in four years, an increase of 19 percent.

Table 4.
Market Policy: Program Crop Domestic and Export Use

Item	:	1982	1983	1984	1985	1986	1987	1988	1989
					- - - million tons - - -				
Domestic Use		229.2	208.9	218.6	233.7	242.1	247.6	250.4	253.3
Exports		124.0	118.9	132.5	128.0	134.6	140.4	149.8	157.1
TOTAL USE		353.2	327.8	351.1	361.7	376.7	388.0	400.2	410.4
Export Value* (billion dollars)					18.9	18.5	19.4	21.2	22.4

* Valued at the farm level price.

The increase in export volume across the program commodities is significant but highly uneven (Table 5). The percentage increase is greatest for rice and least for soybeans.

Table 5.
Market Policy: Program Crop Exports

Commodity	: 1984-85 : : Average :	1986	: :	1987	: :	1988	: :	1989	: 1986-89 : : Average :	% Change
				- - - million tons - - -						
Corn	51.7	53.6		55.3		58.1		59.9	56.7	9.7
Wheat	41.7	44.8		46.1		49.3		52.0	48.1	15.3
Rice	2.9	3.1		3.2		3.4		3.5	3.3	13.8
Soybeans	20.8	22.4		24.8		27.4		29.3	26.0	25.0
Cotton	1.4	1.5		1.5		1.6		1.7	1.6	14.3

Stocks

When the program is implemented at the beginning of 1986, the commodity stocks on hand would be near 105 mmt. This amount would be about 29 percent of combined domestic use and exports, proportionally not nearly as large as in previous times, but probably too much for a market policy.

Thus, quantities owned by the CCC would be reduced, and the size of the farmer-owned reserve would be reduced as far as possible. The burden of maintaining reserves would be shifted to the private sector.

The FOR would decline slightly to 33.4 mmt, while CCC stocks fall to 13.5 mmt (Table 6). These amounts are stable from year to year in this scenario. Bad weather or other shocks would draw the reserves down further. The "free" (that is, privately held) stocks would at first increase as the government-sponsored stocks decline, then fall as well.

Table 6.
Market Policy: Ending Year Commodity Stocks

Commodity	1982	1983	1984	1985	1986	1987	1988	1989
			- - - million tons - - -					
Grains	142.0	73.9	85.6	95.0	85.4	83.1	80.6	78.4
Soybeans	9.4	4.8	6.8	8.5	10.1	10.6	9.4	9.5
Cotton	1.7	0.7	1.0	1.0	1.0	1.0	0.9	0.9
TOTAL	153.1	79.4	93.4	104.5	96.5	94.7	90.7	88.8
Reserve	76.4	31.9	35.2	40.2	33.4	33.4	33.4	33.4
CCC	40.5	13.8	19.6	22.3	13.5	13.5	13.5	13.5
Free	36.2	33.7	38.6	42.0	49.6	47.8	43.8	41.9
TOTAL	153.1	79.4	93.4	104.5	96.5	94.7	90.7	88.8
As % of Domestic & Export Use	43.3	24.2	26.6	28.9	25.6	24.4	22.7	21.6

After initially declining, total stocks would remain relatively constant over this period. As a proportion of total use, the figure for the four years would vary from 22 to 26 percent.

Commodity Prices

With price support floors lowered, the market option results in falling prices for many commodities. For example, corn would average $2.52 per bushel, compared to $2.80 during the four years of the 1981 farm bill (Table 7).

Table 7.
Market Policy: Program Commodity Prices

Commodity	:	1982	:	1983	:	1984	:	1985	:	1986	:	1987	:	1988	:	1989
Corn	:	2.68		3.20		2.68		2.67		2.50		2.51		2.53		2.54
Sorghum	:	2.52		2.75		2.45		2.42		2.22		2.22		2.22		2.22
Barley	:	2.23		2.50		2.35		2.38		2.15		2.15		2.14		2.12
Rye	:	2.41		2.40		2.10		2.30		2.15		2.14		2.12		2.10
Oats	:	1.48		1.69		1.72		1.74		1.55		1.53		1.50		1.45
Wheat	:	3.55		3.54		3.42		3.45		3.20		3.25		3.29		3.32
Rice	:	8.11		8.79		8.30		8.20		7.86		7.80		7.80		8.00
Soybeans	:	5.69		7.75		6.20		6.00		5.60		5.52		5.68		5.67
Cotton	:	59.4		66.4		65.0		67.0		60.0		60.0		65.0		66.0

NOTE: Prices are dollars per bushel except rice (dollars per cwt) and cotton (cents per pound).

Farm Income

The value of the program crop sales shows a slight increase across the four years from 1986 to 1989. The average annual value is almost $51 billion, compared to the 1982-85 average of $49.7 billion, a gain of 3 percent (Table 8).

Table 8.
Market Policy: Value of Program Commodity Production/ Net Farm Income

Item	:	1982	1983	1984	1985	1986	1987	1988	1989
					- - - billion dollars - - -				
Value of Sales		50.5	48.2	50.0	49.9	48.4	49.6	51.7	53.8
Net Farm Income		22.3	16.1	31.0	22.5	20.6	18.5	18.0	17.0

While livestock producers would enjoy favorably priced feed supplies and higher profits, margins for producers of program commodities would be squeezed by lower prices. Income transfers to agriculture would decrease, as would the proportion of total farm income from that source. Net farm income would fall significantly to an average annual rate of $18.5 billion during 1986-1989. The rate of return to investment in agriculture would be insufficient to prevent further deflation of land values.

Program Costs

The primary purpose of this approach is reduced government intervention and smaller commodity programs. Phasing down the programs would substantially lower Treasury outlays, with average annual costs falling to only 22 percent of the amount during the 1981 law (Table 9). Costs in the final three years are less than $400 million.

Table 9.
Market Policy: Program Cost Summary

Item	1982	1983	1984	1985	1986	1987	1988	1989
				- - - million dollars - - -				
Deficiency Payments	1,516.4	2,426.3	3,376.9	3,998.0	2,190.0	48.0	0.0	0.0
Storage	703.1	929.2	354.8	410.0	340.0	340.0	340.0	340.0
Land Diversion	72.0	900.4	677.7	742.0	0.0	0.0	0.0	0.0
TOTAL	2,291.5	4,255.9	4,409.4	5,150.0	2,530.0	388.0	340.0	340.0

With a $20,000 per farmer cap and 15 percent set-asides, deficiency payments would fall almost 45 percent in the first year, and essentially to zero in subsequent years as both target prices and the payment limits are lowered. In the final two years, no target price payments would be made.

The pattern is similar for storage payments. As both FOR and CCC stocks are drawn down, costs decline in the first year and then stabilize. The average annual cost for storage payments is $340 million, about 43 percent below the 1982-85 average.

The savings from paid land diversion would be considerable. These program costs, which averaged $598 million annually under the 1981 law, would be completely eliminated.

Food Prices

This approach would result in slightly lower food prices over the life of the bill. As grain commodity prices trend downward, output in the livestock sector would rise, and prices would fall there as well.

Evaluation

American agriculture has rarely operated within even a quasi-free market regime. As a result, the responses of farmers, foreign purchasers, and others to a greatly changed economic environment can only be approximated. Moreover, the pace of the economic adjustment we anticipate is difficult to predict. The projections of the previous section present a plausible scenario. On that basis, we evaluate the performance of agriculture under this proposal.

Food Safety, Quality, and Prices

The free market approach would not affect the safety and quality of the food supply. Its impact on food prices and consumer expenditures would barely be perceptible.

This approach would eliminate the programs that tend to raise food prices. In the long run, therefore, it would allow consumers to enjoy more of the potential benefits of increasing agricultural productivity. From a consumer perspective, this approach would be viewed as consistent with a national objective of reasonable food prices.

Resource Conservation

There are two considerations in evaluating the effectiveness of the free market approach for conservation: the overall consequences of the changed economic environment; and the adequacy of specific programs addressing resource problems.

During the transition phase, pressures to expand the cropland base and water use would be relieved. The cropland base would probably contract, with marginal land shifted to less intensive uses, and the "sodbuster" provision would keep additional fragile land out of cultivation as long as the programs were in place.

Beyond the transition phase, there would be no programs that would spur cultivation of unsuitable land. In circumstances of worldwide supply shortages, however, free market agriculture would not preclude sudden, massive expansion onto fragile lands.

The effectiveness of conservation programs would depend upon the way they were administered. If current programs were targeted toward the most erosion-prone land, erosion would be reduced—even at existing funding levels. However, if the programs were continued as presently administered, they would be much less effective. At the very least, the commodity programs would no longer be operating at cross-purposes with resource conservation efforts.

91

Farm Income and Structure

1. Farm income

Through the transition phase, farm income under the free market approach would be substantially lower than under current policy. Additional disinvestment would occur as higher returns available in other sectors drew capital away from agriculture. At some point, returns from agricultural investment would again equal those from the overall economy (as has been the case over the long run). Thus, the free market approach is not necessarily inconsistent with acceptable levels of farm income. But it is the adjustment during the transition—the magnitude of capital losses and their victims—that poses the problem.

2. Farm structure

The free market policy would have significant effects on the structure of agriculture. Reduced government income transfers would increase the financial pressures now being experienced by many commercial farms, as would lower commodity prices. Reduced farm incomes would call the survival of many farms into question and would increase the failure rate.

It is not altogether clear how the assets of failed farms would be redistributed. Lower land values could make it easier for young people to enter farming, and the number and average size of farms firms could be largely unchanged after the shakeout. This scenario is improbable, however. It is more likely that existing farmers with strong balance sheets would be in the best position to buy out failed farms. By the time agriculture had completed the transition to greater reliance on the market, there would probably be fewer commercial farms of larger average size. This trend would undoubtedly hurt many rural businesses and communities to some extent.

Over the long run, the free market approach would promote an agricultural structure primarily determined by technological change and increasing productivity.

Economic Growth and Competitiveness

1. Stability

The effect of the free market approach on the stability of agriculture is unclear. It could be argued that after the transition, farmers would respond more incrementally to the factors that fuel booms and busts, thus reducing the severity of the swings. This argument holds that government policy spurred the boom and exacerbated the bust during the 1970s-1980s cycle. Market signals that indicated oncoming decline were masked by price and income supports. Rather than being gradually reduced over several seasons, production continued apace. As a result, large stocks accumulated (reaching

43 percent of domestic and export use in 1982), forcing the government to institute the highly disruptive (and expensive) PIK program. Had incremental annual adjustments been made in response to the market, it is argued, this swing would have been dampened.

Under free market policies, shifts in supply or demand that pushed prices sharply higher would at first bring the commodity reserves into play. If prices remained strong, farmers would expand plantings and output in the next season, leading to rising asset values if demand and prices met expectations.

But what would happen when an economic downturn began? Would farmers attempt to use their political clout to secure govenment intervention to prevent declining prices and asset values? Without government programs propping up agriculture, would adjustment occur slowly enough to avoid sector-wide problems? Experience with these possibilities is so limited that answers are necessarily speculative.

In the absence of current government programs, prices could move sharply lower (because of the lack of effective supports) or higher (because of reduced reserves). It is not inconceivable that another 1970s-type environment could develop, creating expectations similar to those that fueled the earlier boom. Nor is it impossible for conditions to emerge that would again burst the expansionary bubble. Such events would almost certainly multiply political pressures to scrap the market-oriented policies in order to ameliorate the plight of farmers, bankers, rural communities, farm and food related industries, and others.

Thus, the effects of free market policies on agricultural stability might well be mixed. Within the boundaries of "normal" circumstances, these policies would probably increase stability by encouraging smaller, more frequent adjustments. In extraordinary circumstances, however, these policies might actually diminish the stability of commodity prices and farm incomes.

2. Exports

The free market approach would tend to expand U.S. agricultural exports, as reductions in price and income supports enhanced the competitiveness of our products. But realizing the full benefits of this policy would take time because of offsetting forces such as the high value of the dollar and the protectionist practices of other nations.

Adoption of this approach, however, would clearly signal a new American trade posture and significantly increase the pressure on our competitors. Over time, it would probably force them to modify their trade policies. For example, our refusal to continue floor prices through supports and production controls could substantially increase the cost of the EEC's Common Agricultural Policy. Their export subsidies would have to be increased to maintain their market share, and the pressures on an already strained budget would quickly build. In addition, it would be easier to grant foreign producers greater access to our markets in return for similar action on their part. The overall result in future years could be more open global trade and increased responsiveness of world markets to considerations of efficiency and price.

Foreign Responsibilities

The effects of free market policies on Third World agricultural development would be mixed. In the short run, lower priced commodities would prove beneficial to the food-deficit countries, helping hold down their import bills and conserving use of scarce foreign exchange. The other side, of course, is that the availability of cheap food reduces incentives for indigenous agricultural development.

To the extent that developing countries could take advantage of greater access to our markets, the policy would be beneficial. The expanded exports of these countries would generate additional foreign exchange earnings, expanding their domestic growth and increasing their ability to buy our products.

The impact of this policy on humanitarian food assistance would be small. While surplus commodity stocks in government stores would be lower, the international emergency food reserve would remain, and open market purchases could be used to supplement them as needed. With reduced expenditures for other agriculture programs, budgetary pressures would be eased, and adequate funding for humanitarian aid would probably be forthcoming.

Overall, the free market policy would be consistent with an expanded role for U.S. agriculture in strengthening food production and consumption in the rest of the world while promoting our national interests as well.

SELECTED REFERENCES

Economic Report of the President. U.S. Government Printing Office, Washington, D.C., February 1984.

Bruce Gardner, *The Governing of Agriculture.* Lawrence, Kansas, The Regents Press of Kansas, 1981.

Elaine S. Grigsby and Cathy L. Jabara, "Agricultural Export Programs and U.S. Agriculture Policy." *Agricultural-Food Policy Review,* Economic Research Service, USDA, forthcoming.

Harold Malmgren, "A Strategic Response to Global Competition," in PTFIPE Selected Papers, December 1984.

The President's Task Force on International Private Enterprise, *Report to the President*. Washington, D.C., December 1984.

The President's Task Force on International Private Enterprise, *Selected Papers,* December 1984.

U.S. Department of Agriculture, *Agricultural Adjustment Act of 1985*, February 1985.

Chapter 8

Restricted Production

Introduction

Directly opposed to the free market approach are policies that involve extensive government management of the balance between food supply and food use. Support for this approach, largely confined to farm groups, varies with economic conditions, intensifying in times of abundant supplies and low prices. It received serious attention in the late 1970s when it was strongly espoused by a newly formed farm organization, the American Agriculture Movement (AAM). Today, the four-year recession in the farm economy has sparked renewed interest.

Those who propose production control as the centerpiece of farm policy see excess supply as the fundamental problem of agriculture. They suggest that under normal conditions, American agriculture has the capacity to produce far more than is needed for domestic and foreign markets, resulting in prices below many farmers' costs of production and a continued economic squeeze. They argue that recent efforts to remedy this imbalance by expanding demand (primarily in foreign markets) has proved unsuccessful and has left farmers even more vulnerable to political fluctuations such as embargoes and protectionism. Moreover, they suggest, current programs work to the disadvantage of farmers by permitting or even stimulating overproduction.

After four consecutive years of negative returns on equity investment, rising debt-to-aset ratios, and inadequate cash flow, advocates of production controls believe that it is fruitless to tinker with current programs. Instead, they argue that radical steps must be taken to assure farmers returns at least equivalent to their cost of production plus a "reasonable" profit from the marketplace. To do this, agriculture must be insulated from the effects of fiscal, monetary, and trade policies beyond its control. The most feasible way to accomplish this, they conclude, is to regulate production.

Support for this approach also reflects the reality that large federal subsidies for agriculture cannot be sustained politically. When the books are closed in the fall of 1985, the 1981 farm bill will probably have cost taxpayers more than all the commodity programs for the previous 18 years. Policy deliberations in 1985 will surely seek to reduce these costs significantly. Thus, rather than continuing farmers' dependence on uncertain government payments, this approach seeks to safeguard and even enlarge benefits by shifting costs from taxpayers to consumers.

In arguing for this shift, proponents note that Americans pay a smaller percentage of their incomes for food than do consumers in most other nations. From this fact, they infer that our concluding consumers would be willing to pay more to ensure a healthy farm economy. Moreover, they argue that, spread across all consumers in our society, the burden imposed on individual consumers would not be excessive.

This approach is also said to promote the survival of small and medium-size commercial family farms, thereby contributing to the vitality of rural communities and the preservation of America's cultural heritage. Proponents argue that without the enhanced assistance that only production controls can provide, many family farms will be forced out of business and swallowed up by larger operations, concentrating production even further. They note that many of these farms are quite efficient and that society gains little in higher productivity or lower food prices from their demise. In fact, they argue that society incurs a net cost when farmers are driven off their land, both because the economic base of rural America is eroded and because burdens on urban areas, already staggering under high unemployment and declining tax bases, are further increased.

Another argument for this approach is that it would alleviate much of the financial stress on farmers and lenders stemming from declining asset values. Substantially higher commodity prices, increasing farmers' cash flow, would push land values higher, perhaps even returning them to the peaks of the 1970s.

This approach is also said to conserve resources and protect the environment. Proponents of production controls argue that the expansion of production to meet foreign demand could well inflict lasting damage on our soil. They cite the increased cultivation of fragile lands, greater use of fertilizers, chemicals, and energy, and the unaffordability of soil conservation practices for many farmers. They contend that it makes no sense to deplete our soil and water resources, polluting streams and water tables, just to export ever-greater quantities at ever-lower prices to nations that could well afford to pay considerably more. If production were restricted, the pressure to expand cultivation to fragile lands and to farm existing acres too intensively would be greatly reduced. The most erosive acres could be taken out of production, and with higher incomes farmers could afford to implement sound conservation practices.

Finally, proponents of this approach argue that it provides greater certainty and stability for farmers and for the rest of the food system. Farmers would know in advance how much of each crop to produce, and the possibility of sudden, wide price swings would be substantially reduced.

Description of the Program

Farm programs of the past 50 years included considerable experience with supply and marketing management, in the form of allotments and quotas. From this experience, coupled with a range of current proposals, we have assembled a policy package that would implement production controls.

Participation and Compliance

In recent times, supply management programs have been voluntary, with program benefits providing the incentive to participate. But these incentives have proved to be unaffordable. Proposals that seek to avoid high budget costs must therefore rest on some form of mandatory compliance. Typically, this would involve submitting production control proposals to affected farmers in referenda. If those voting approve by the specified majority, compliance would be required for all farmers.

Commodity Coverage

The commodities that would be included in this proposal are the major field crops (storable commodities) covered by current programs. Livestock would be excluded, for three reasons. Livestock never has been covered; attempting to include it would guarantee irresistable political opposition to the restricted production approach; and few proponents of restricted production now propose to include it. As we shall see, however, excluding livestock leads to significant stresses within the agricultural sector.

Price Targets and Guarantees

The principal aim of this approach is to increase farmers' incomes and returns on their investments by specifying and guaranteeing commodity prices. Proposals to do this typically relate desired prices to parity or to farmers' cost of production. In 1978, the AAM called for 100 percent of parity prices; other proposals have called for prices that cover all production costs plus a ''reasonable'' profit.

In the proposal examined here, the price guarantees are set at levels that cover production costs for most crops, equivalent to about 70 percent of the full parity price (Table 1). Total cost of production includes a return to the principal fixed asset, land. (It is through this return that the guaranteed price levels influence long-run asset values.) These price targets average roughly 45 percent above current commodity prices (Table 2).

Table 1.
Commodity Production Costs in Relation to Parity Prices

| Commodity | : | Three-Year Average Cost of Production | | : | : Parity Price : | 70 Percent |
	:	Excluding Land	: Total	:	: January 1985 :	of Parity
Corn		2.27	2.89		5.14	3.60
Sorghum		2.57	3.09		4.86	3.40
Barley		2.43	3.01		4.76	3.33
Oats		1.89	2.44		3.03	2.12
Wheat		3.25	4.17		7.07	4.95
Rice		8.13	9.61		19.60	13.72
Soybeans		4.42	6.45		12.80	8.96
Cotton		64.3	75.3		12.4	87.0

NOTE: All prices are dollars per bushels except rice (dollars per cwt) and cotton (cents per pound).

Table 2.
Parity Prices in Relation to Market Prices

Commodity	:	January 1985 Market Price	:	70 Percent of Parity	:	Percent Difference
Corn		2.53		3.60		42.3
Sorghum		2.30		3.40		47.8
Barley		2.26		3.33		47.3
Oats		1.69		2.12		25.4
Wheat		3.74		4.95		32.3
Rice		8.14		13.72		68.6
Soybeans		6.10		8.96		46.9
Cotton		57.0		87.0		52.6

NOTE: All prices are dollars per bushels except rice (dollars per cwt) and cotton (cents per pound).

The price guarantee would be adjusted in years beyond 1986 to maintain a comparable relation to total production costs. The prevailing parity price and projected price guarantees are shown in Table 3.

100

Table 3.
Commodity Parity Prices and Projected Price Guarantees

Commodity	Parity Price		70 Percent of Parity Price*			
	Jan. 1985	Jan. 1986*	1986	1987	1988	1989
Corn	5.14	5.35	3.74	3.89	4.05	4.21
Sorghum	4.86	5.05	3.54	3.68	3.83	3.98
Barley	4.76	4.95	3.47	3.60	3.75	3.90
Oats	3.30	3.15	2.21	2.29	2.39	2.48
Wheat	7.07	7.35	5.15	5.35	5.57	5.79
Rice	19.60	20.38	14.27	14.84	15.43	16.05
Soybeans	12.80	13.31	9.32	9.69	10.08	10.48
Cotton	124	129	90	94	98	102

NOTE: All prices are dollars per bushels except rice (dollars per cwt) and cotton (cents per pound). *Forecast. Assumed to increase four percent annually.

Mechanisms for Achieving Price Targets

The guaranteed prices would be achieved through the CCC nonrecourse loan program. That is, the guarantees are loan rates, with the CCC standing ready to purchase all quantities of the commodity at the loan price. But without limits on available quantities, the CCC would quickly be purchasing huge, unaffordable amounts. Thus, supply must be restricted enough to ensure that the market price is above the guaranteed price so that commodities go into the market rather than to the CCC.

This would require production controls, managed as follows. First, a national acreage base would be established by inventorying actual plantings in recent years. Once this is done, the national base would then be apportioned equitably to individual producers. For each farmer, allowable production in any future year would be some fraction of that base, determined by the amount of production deemed necessary to meet domestic and export needs.

Each year, well before planting time, USDA would project the quantity of each commodity needed in the coming year to meet domestic, export, and stockholding needs. This would be translated into the national acreage required (based on national average yields), and then apportioned to individual farmers in the form of some percentage of their farm cropland base. (Some proposals have suggested apportionment by a sliding scale that would give preferential treatment to smaller farmers by allowing them to cultivate more of their base acreage. For example, farms with a base of say 300 acres would be allowed to plant 75 percent while a farm with a base of 600 acres would be allowed only 60 percent.) In addition to an acreage allotment or base, each farmer would be given a quota (corresponding to expected production from the base acreage) limiting the amount that may be marketed.

With domestic commodity prices pushed considerably above world market prices, domestic users would attempt to turn to cheaper foreign supplies. But imports would undermine the program, making it impossible to achieve the price guarantees. It would therefore be necessary to curb imports by establishing quotas, levying duties and fees, or requiring that imports sell for some set amount above the guaranteed price.

Commodity Reserves

To provide for variations in weather and yield, a contingency reserve is included in this proposal, with a maximum size based on percentages of total annual use—10 percent for feed grains and 20 percent for food grains. The stocks would remain under farmer ownership with an extended CCC loan and a storage subsidy provided for up to three years. A release price would be established at 115 percent of the guaranteed price. That is, if market prices rose to this level, the storage subsidy would cease and the loans would have to be repaid.

Soil Conservation

This proposal would require that land taken out of cultivation be treated in a manner consistent with sound conservation practices.

Performance of Agriculture under Production Controls

Adjustment

Under this approach, the economic performance of the farm sector would differ sharply from that experienced during the past 15 years. Restricting the production by the amount required to achieve an almost 50 percent increase in commodity prices would require considerable adjustment and a fair amount of administrative trial and error. Economic adjustments would be required, not only for crop farmers, who must change the scale of their operations, but also for livestock producers, who would suddenly be confronted with sharply higher feed costs. The adjustments would extend to the farm supply industries facing a significantly reduced market for their products, the export industry facing sharply lower volume, the food processing and marketing industries facing a shifting price structure, and to consumers facing higher food costs.

102

Production

The program would begin with determination of the expected domestic and export use for 1986, taking into account the stocks that are carried forward from 1985, some of which must be moved into the market. Since both domestic and foreign purchasers would respond to higher prices by purchasing considerably less, production in the first year would have to be reduced substantially. Total production of only 296 mmt would prove sufficient to meet the market needs (Table 4). This quantity is some 75 mmt, 20 percent, below the production expected in 1985.

Table 4.
Restricted Production Policy:
Program Crop Acreage and Production

Item	:	1982	1983	1984	1985	1986	1987	1988	1989
				— — — million acres — — —					
Area Planted		295.7	248.3	284.5	280.3	209.5	206.4	201.4	198.2
Area Idled		10.7	75.6	29.9	25.9	103.1	106.2	111.2	114.4
TOTAL (Base Acreage)		306.4	323.9	314.4	306.2	312.6	312.6	312.6	312.6
% Idled		3.5	23.3	9.5	8.9	33.0	34.0	35.6	36.6
				— — — million tons — — —					
Production		395.2	253.3	364.5	383.4	274.0	300.0	295.1	292.7
				— — —tons — — —					
Production/ Acre		1.34	1.02	1.28	1.32	1.41	1.43	1.46	1.48

In a normal weather year, this level of production could be obtained with plantings of no more than 210 million acres, 71 million fewer acres than will be planted in 1985. From a national acreage base for these commodities of 312.6 million acres, plantings of this amount would require 103 million acres (33.0 percent) of that base to be idled. This means that the average farm would be allowed to plant only 67.0 percent of its base acreage, with the remaining acreage devoted to mandatory soil conservation. (The apportionment of the national base acreage among farms could be scaled to allow proportionately more of the base for smaller farms. This would not appreciably affect overall estimates, however.)

103

The proportion of farmland that must be idled to maintain the price targets would vary in subsequent years. However, it would average 35 percent over the four years. Production would be relatively constant across the period.

In previous episodes of acreage reduction, yields have accelerated because farmers idle their least productive land and cultivate the remaining acreage more intensively by greater application of fertilizers and pesticides. The huge acreage restrictions in the proposed program would therefore tend to produce rapid yield increases.

Given these assumptions about acreage and yields, production would average 295 mmt, 20 percent less than the average output of the 1984-85 seasons. Achieving the price targets would thus require reducing production by one-fifth and idling well over one-third of the productive base acreage.

Domestic and Export Use

Faced with much higher commodity prices, domestic and foreign consumers would respond by sharply curtailing their use (Table 5.) In the domestic market, use in the first year would decline almost 23 mmt (10 percent) from the previous year. This would be reflected in less livestock feeding, grain and oilseed use, and industrial consumption. Over the four years 1986-89, the average use in the domestic market would be 209 mmt, 8 percent below the average for 1984-85.

Table 5.
Restricted Production Policy:
Program Crop Domestic and Export Use

Item	:	1982	1983	1984	1985	1986	1987	1988	1989
				— — — million tons — — —					
Domestic									
Use		229.2	208.9	218.6	233.7	210.9	209.9	208.7	207.6
Exports		124.0	118.9	132.5	128.0	100.1	98.0	95.9	93.9
TOTAL USE		353.2	327.8	351.1	361.7	311.0	307.9	304.6	301.5
Export									
Value*					18.9	21.8	22.2	22.6	23.1
(billion dollars)									

* Valued at the farm level price.

Export demand would likewise fall precipitously, from 128.0 mmt in 1985 to 100 mmt in 1986, a decline of 22 percent in the first year. Over the four years, exports would average about 97 mmt per year, 26 percent below the already depressed amounts for 1984-85. The reduction varies considerably across the program commodities because of the differing demand elasticities for each crop (Table 6). Feed grain exports would be most affected, cotton the least.

Although the export volume is reduced by almost one-fourth (Table 5), this decline would be more than offset by higher prices. In the first year, the value of sales abroad would rise 15 percent. Over the four years, sales would average $22.4 billion, 19 percent higher than in 1985.

Table 6.
Restricted Production Policy:
Program Crop Exports

Commodity	: 1984-85 : : Average :	1986	:	1987	:	1988	:	1989	: 1986-89 : : Average :	% Change
				— — — million tons — — —						
Corn	51.7	40.8		39.9		38.9		38.0	39.4	−23.8
Wheat	41.7	33.7		33.1		32.5		31.9	32.8	−21.3
Rice	2.9	2.2		2.2		2.2		2.1	2.2	−24.1
Soybeans	20.8	15.7		15.4		15.1		14.8	15.3	−26.4
Cotton	1.4	1.2		1.2		1.2		1.1	1.2	−14.3

Combined domestic and export use would fall to an average of 306 mmt in 1986-89 from the average of 356 mmt in 1984-85, a decline of 14 percent.

Stocks

At the beginning of the 1986 crop year, commodity stocks are expected to total 105 mmt. Under the restricted production approach, this amount would be excessive, because less inventory is needed for the smaller domestic and export usage. Stocks would therefore be reduced by returning them to the market and reducing annual production commensurately. Restricting production in 1986 by drawing down stocks could reduce the end-of-year holdings by 15 percent, to 89 mmt. Stocks would be held near this level in subsequent years. Over the four years, annual stocks would average 72 mmt, equivalent to 23 percent of combined domestic and export use, somewhat less than in recent years (Table 7.)

Table 7.
Restricted Production Policy:
Ending Year Commodity Stocks

Commodity	1982	1983	1984	1985	1986	1987	1988	1989
	— — — million tons — — —							
Grains	142.0	73.9	85.6	95.0	80.6	67.9	58.5	52.0
Soybeans	9.4	4.8	6.8	8.5	8.0	7.2	5.8	4.7
Cotton	1.7	0.7	1.0	1.2	0.6	0.7	0.7	0.8
TOTAL	153.1	79.4	93.4	104.5	89.2	75.8	65.0	57.5
Reserve	76.4	31.9	35.2	40.2	35.3	27.4	19.4	14.0
CCC	40.5	13.8	19.6	22.3	8.8	8.8	8.8	8.3
Free	36.2	33.7	38.6	42.0	45.1	39.6	36.8	35.2
TOTAL	153.1	79.4	93.4	104.5	89.2	75.8	65.0	57.5
As % of Domestic & Export Use	43.3	24.2	26.6	28.9	28.7	24.6	21.3	19.1

Commodity Prices

For the most part, commodity prices would be administered and known in advance (Table 8). They would vary little except when bad weather caused unexpected declines in output. In that event, prices would begin to move above the target levels but would be slowed by releasing reserves and CCC stocks onto the market. They also would be dampened by the knowledge that the acreage base could be expanded in subsequent years to increase production and rebuild stocks. (This same pattern would apply to sudden surges in foreign demand.) A combination of reduced domestic production and a surge in export demand so strong that the reserves were insufficient to stem price rises would however raise unpopular questions about export limitations.

106

Table 8.
Restricted Production Policy:
Program Commodity Prices

Commodity	1982	1983	1984	1985	1986	1987	1988	1989
Corn	2.68	3.20	2.68	2.67	3.74	3.89	4.05	4.21
Sorghum	2.52	2.75	2.45	2.42	3.54	3.68	3.83	3.98
Barley	2.23	2.50	2.35	2.38	3.47	3.60	3.75	3.90
Rye	2.41	2.40	2.10	2.30	3.52	3.66	3.81	3.96
Oats	1.48	1.69	1.72	1.74	2.21	2.29	2.39	2.48
Wheat	3.55	3.54	3.42	3.45	5.15	5.35	5.57	5.79
Rice	8.11	8.79	8.30	8.20	14.27	14.84	15.43	16.05
Soybeans	5.69	7.75	6.20	6.00	9.32	9.69	10.00	10.48
Cotton	59.4	66.4	65.0	67.0	90.0	94.0	98.0	102.0

NOTE: Prices are dollars per bushel except rice (dollars per cwt) and cotton (cents per pound).

Farm Income

The overall farm income picture would be mixed in both the short and the long run. Producers of controlled commodities would experience rising incomes, even though they would be producing and marketing considerably less. Over the four years, the value of their sales would average almost $60 billion, an increase of 20 percent over the $50 billion average for 1984-85 (Table 9).

Table 9.
Restricted Production Policy:
Value of Program Commodity Production/Net Farm Income

Item	1982	1983	1984	1985	1986	1987	1988	1989
				— — — billion dollars — — —				
Value of Sales	50.5	48.2	50.0	49.9	53.7	60.5	61.8	63.7
Net Farm Income	22.3	16.1	31.0	32.5	25.1	26.1	26.6	27.4

While the net incomes of producers covered by this program would be considerably higher, these gains would be offset to some extent by the effects on other producers. Initially, livestock producers would experience lower incomes because of higher costs and lower prices. Confronted with much higher feed prices, they would begin adjusting, reducing their use of

107

feed by liquidating their breeding herds. As more animals were marketed, livestock prices would fall, reducing gross revenues while increasing the quantity of meat products on the market. In the first year, lower livestock revenues would offset the higher revenues for crop farmers, so that net farm income would be little changed. After a few years, livestock producers would adjust to higher feed prices and production would again rise. However, both livestock and meat prices would be higher, reflecting the changed cost structure for the industry.

Net farm income in 1986-89 would average $26.3 billion, an increase of about 14 percent over the average for the 1982-85 period. Beyond the first four years, after adjustment in the livestock industry had been completed, net incomes for this generation of farmers would be expected to remain higher, by as much as 20 percent.

Program Costs

This approach would reduce budget costs considerably. In fact, the only costs would be for administration and the storage subsidy associated with stockholdings. Storage costs for both the reserve and CCC inventories would average just over $246 million annually (Table 10).

Table 10.
Restricted Production Policy:
Program Cost Summary

Item	1982	1983	1984	1985	1986	1987	1988	1989
			— — — million dollars — — —					
Deficiency Payments	1,516.4	2,426.3	3,376.9	3,998.0	0.0	0.0	0.0	0.0
Storage	703.1	929.2	354.8	410.0	359.0	278.0	199.0	146.0
Land Diversion	72.0	900.4	677.7	742.0	0.0	0.0	0.0	0.0
TOTAL	2,291.5	4,255.9	4,409.4	5,150.0	359.0	278.0	199.0	146.0

Food Prices

While this approach would greatly reduce taxpayers' costs, it shifts much of the cost to consumers through higher food prices. The pattern of those prices would be closely related to the pace of adjustment in the livestock sector.

Initially, the abrupt change in commodity prices would rapidly increase consumer food prices. The commodity price rise in the first year would average 42 percent for approximately 30 percent of the value of all farm products. This would produce an increase in the index of all farm product prices of about 13 percent, which would be translated into a food price increase of about 4.0 percent, adding about 0.8 percent to the general rate of inflation as measured by the CPI.

The experience in the second year would be different. By then, as herds were liquidated, much greater quantities of meat products would be on the market, driving down retail prices. This would offset much if not all of the upward price pressure from higher crop prices.

By the third year, much of the adjustment in the livestock sector would be completed. The quantities of meat and dairy products on the market would be lower, and their prices would rise. This would produce a second surge in food prices so that in the fourth year, consumers would feel the full effects of both higher grain and higher livestock prices. As food prices rose, consumers would respond by shifting their demand among various products. The present downward trend in consumption of meat and dairy products would accelerate.

Additional consumer costs over four years might approximate $45 billion. In subsequent years, consumer food prices would stabilize at higher levels (perhaps as much as eight percent above 1985), increasing aggregate food expenditures by about $25 billion annually.

Evaluation

This approach diverges widely from the experience of recent times. Nevertheless, the general direction and magnitude of its effects can be ascertained with some confidence.

Food Safety, Quality, and Prices

This approach would produce no perceptible changes in the safety and quality of the nation's food policy. Its effect on the food price goal would be perceptible, however. The "reasonableness" of food prices is to some extent a subjective judgment. But if the present level of food prices is considered reasonable, then the increase that would result from this proposal would be in conflict with that objective. If, however, present food prices are thought to be unfairly low, then the increase would be compatible with it.

Another way of evaluating this issue is to compare the additional cost to consumers with the benefits gained by farmers. If farmers benefitted in direct proportion to increased consumer costs, the policy would at least be an effective transfer mechanism. If consumer costs are much greater than farmer benefits, then this would be an inefficient means of improving the economic status of farmers. In fact, as we have seen, added annual costs to consumers would be far in excess of increases in net farm income.

The impact of higher food prices on different sectors of the population is also significant. Higher prices are relatively more burdensome for low income consumers. If this burden were alleviated through public food assistance programs, government costs would rise. To the extent that this occurs, the policy would impose an added indirect cost on taxpayers.

Overall, given the skewed distribution of benefits to farmers, the significant increase in food expenditures, the high cost to consumers relative to farmer benefits, and added burdens on poorer Americans and taxpayers, this approach cannot be viewed as wholly compatible with the goal of "reasonable" food prices.

Resource Conservation

For decades it was believed that government production control programs, which idled cropland, contributed significantly to the control of soil erosion. It was assumed that the land farmers elected to idle was among the most highly erosive and that requiring sound conservation practices (e.g., cover crops) reduced the erosion rate. Recently, however, more comprehensive information on soil erosion has called this assumption into question. The most erosive or potentially erosive land may not be idled, compliance with required conservation practices may not be very extensive, and these practices may not be very effective. Thus, it can no longer be assumed that idling land, even as much as 100 million acres, would resolve the erosion problem.

But idling the amount of land contemplated in the restricted production approach would undoubtedly reduce the magnitude and severity of the problem. With the addition of specifically focused measures and regulations, the overall effectiveness of this policy could be greatly increased. To the extent that erosion and associated problems such as stream pollution are reduced, society as a whole would benefit.

This approach by its very nature would relieve various pressures on the land. It would reduce the need for continual expansion of the cropland base, which frequently extends to "fragile" lands. It would minimize the probability of boom and bust swings, which induce neglect of conservation practices and side effects detrimental to the environment. By the same token, this approach would relieve pressure on water resources. Reduced production would require less irrigation and slow the depletion of underground water sources. It would lessen competition for the available surface supplies and eliminate the need to move large volumes of water at great expense to semi-arid areas.

110

Overall, this approach would contribute to the long-term conservation of the nation's natural resources.

Farm Income and Structure

1. Farm Income

The restricted production approach would significantly affect farm incomes, with many farmers experiencing increased returns. But the distribution of benefits across agriculture would be highly uneven. Owners of the land producing crops covered by the program at the time the policy was implemented would be the primary beneficiaries. With their costs little changed but receipts from sales substantially increased, operating margins would be appreciably higher. Other farmers, particlarly livestock farmers, would see their returns reduced in the short run, and even after adjustment, would be unlikely to earn returns above earlier levels. On balance, higher returns to crop producers would probably outweigh lower returns to livestock producers, raising aggregate net farm income.

This approach would, however, have little effect on the long-run rate of return on investment in the farm sector. The generation of farmers owning land at the time the programs are instituted would receive higher returns. Their right to produce higher priced commodities would quickly raise the value of their land. Sale of land at the higher price would provide the original owner a windfall capital gain. But subsequent purchasers of that land would face higher costs and lower profit margins. The much larger capital outlays needed to enter farming would reduce return on investment to roughly the levels prevailing before the restricted production approach was adopted.

2. Farm Structure

In the short run, the economic health and viability of existing farmers would be improved by production controls. Many commercial crop farmers now experiencing inadequate cash flow and sagging land values would have their financial position buttressed by an average 45 percent increase in commodity prices. Cash flow would suddenly increase, improving their ability to service long-term debt and meet short-term operating costs. The decline in asset values would be halted and perhaps even reversed. In fact, this approach would ease much of the financial distress that now besets many farmers and threatens to engulf still others in the years just ahead. To the extent that reducing farm failures slows the process of consolidation into fewer larger farms, this policy would promote the goal of preserving the "family farm."

But the effects are not uniformly positive across the agricultural sector. Increased returns to crop farmers come at the expense of livestock produc-

111

ers. The financial position of these producers would be eroded, perhaps to the point of increasing business failures and hastening consolidation.

In the longer run, the picture is quite different, because the positive effects of this approach are unlikely to extend beyond the present generation. The survival of the next generation of farmers, whose costs would be shifted upward by higher land values, would be placed in jeopardy, and long-term rates of failure and attrition would then resume.

In addition, this approach would have a very considerable impact on the rural economy, of which farming is but a part. This policy would require the idling of almost two-fifths of the nation's cropland base. The ripple effects would be severe. Fertilizer, chemical, and machinery use would be reduced by as much as $15 billion annually, affecting not only manufacturing profits and employment, but also local distribution and service networks. Local financial institutions would see their lending volume reduced. Moreover, there is a rural infrastructure that has become dependent on high volume. Under stiff production controls, local grain elevators, cotton gins, and many other services would be underutilized, leading to capital losses and reduced employment. Effects such as these were starkly evident from the PIK program, which idled only three-fourths as much land as would this approach, and only for one year.

Economic Growth and Competitiveness

1. Stability

In the short term, the controlled production approach would increase stability by reducing the volatility of prices and shifting risks from individual farmers to the government. (At the same time, of course, it would reduce the rewards stemming from individual innovation and entrepreneurship.)

This approach would also reduce longer term, cyclical instability by greatly reducing the dependence of agricultural producers on volatile foreign markets and by offering farmers guaranteed protection against downside risks. But while "busts" are virtually ruled out, "booms" would still be possible. A combination of supply/demand conditions could occur such that the reserves and CCC stocks would not be enough to prevent extremely high prices. On the other hand, a long period of higher prices would be unlikely, because the release of additional lands for cultivation in the next season could bring prices down again. Overall, agriculture would be far less vulnerable to the wide price cycles that bring rapidly inflating land values and overinvestment, only to be followed by declining asset values and disinvestment.

2. Exports

The strict production control approach would reverse the export policy followed over the past 15 years. Rather than attempting to increase foreign sales by expanding existing markets and developing new ones, U.S. policy would turn inward to focus on supporting internal commodity prices. The loss of export volume would be some 20 percent, with a corresponding reduction in the U.S. share of world food trade. However, administered prices would be high enough that even with lower volume, total export earnings would increase. If U.S. agricultural imports grew at historical trend rates or less, the contribution of agriculture to the nation's trade balance would be even greater than in recent years.

While export revenues would rise, the export industry would suffer. Capacity expanded substantially in the 1970s. With reduced volume, much of that capacity would go unused, resulting in considerable capital losses. Employment in export industries is also linked to volume, and the loss of jobs would be significant. Over the long run, this policy would preclude growth in the export industry, thus reducing the role of agriculture in the national economy.

Foreign Responsibilities

The effects of production control policies on agricultural development in developing countries are mixed. In the short term, it would prove disadvantageous to those countries, which would suddenly be confronted with much higher prices for the food they must import to meet the requirements of domestic consumption. For those countries already seriously short of hard currency, an increasing import bill would only add to their difficulties. Moreover, it could direct scarce capital away from long-term agricultural investment to finance short-term import needs. This policy would also reduce the ability of these countries to earn investment dollars through trade, because the import barriers needed to protect U.S. production controls would restrict access to our domestic market.

In the short run, therefore, the approach would exacerbate the problems of developing countries. This approach would also negate one of the key premises for encouraging third world development—that more rapid development leads to higher incomes and a greater overall volume of trade, which is beneficial to all participants and especially to the United States. By effectively precluding U.S. agriculture from sharing in global trade expansion, this policy would reduce our self-interest in promoting the development of poorer countries.

Over the longer term, the impact of this policy would be more positive. The much higher costs of U.S. food imports would increase the incentive of developing countries to expand their own production. Import-substitution policies would become more attractive, encouraging sounder policies and greater investment in agriculture. Higher prices would also encourage some

113

countries to produce for export as a means of earning sorely needed foreign exchange.

This approach would increase political resistance to direct food aid. Budget allocations for this purpose expand only slowly. Because surplus commodities would be less readily available, increased quantities would have to be purchased in the market at the higher prices. Maintaining the present volume of food aid through PL 480, let alone expanding it, would require increased funding. This could prove difficult at times when budgetary concerns are paramount, as is now the case. Much the same argument holds for emergency food assistance.

SELECTED REFERENCES

Council for Agricultural Science and Technology, *The Emerging Economics of Agriculture: Review and Policy Options.* Report No. 98, Ames, Iowa, September 1983.

D. Gale Johnson, "The Performance of Past Policies: A Critique." Paper presented at the Conference on Alternative Agricultural and Food Policies and the 1985 Farm Bill, Berkeley, California, June 11-12, 1984.

Tim Phipps, "Farm Policies and the Rate of Return on Investment in Agriculture." Occasional Papers, American Enterprise Institute, Washington, D.C., November 1984.

Texas Department of Agriculture, *A Populist Proposal to Save America's Family Farms.* Austin, Texas, 1984.

U.S. Department of Agriculture, *Analysis of American Agricultural Movement Proposal.* Issue Briefing Paper, Washington, D.C., March 1978.

Chapter 9

Mixed Reform

Introduction

The approaches to agricultural policy discussed in the preceding two chapters—the free market and restricted production control—rest on the belief that the continuation of current policy imposes excessive burdens on taxpayers without bringing adequate benefits to farmers. The approach discussed in this chapter—what we call the strategy of "mixed reform"—also accepts that belief. But it differs from the other proposals for change in one crucial respect. The mixed reform approach rejects the proposition that any single overall policy can adequately further the many diverse agricultural goals that we wish to achieve. Instead, mixed reform seeks to combine a variety of narrower subpolicies—each designed to attack a specific problem—into a coherent whole.

This approach rests on five key premises.

First, agriculture is unique in several respects. Its vulnerability to unpredictable natural forces and its dependence on erratic international markets generate an instability that is inherent and unavoidable. This instability justifies continuing, long-term efforts by the government to dampen cyclical swings and to compensate for their effects.

Second, the agricultural sector includes but is not restricted to farmers. Rural businesses and communities, manufacturers of farm equipment and other imports, food processors and exporters—all these groups (and others) must be taken fairly into account in designing programs. We need a national food and agriculture policy, not just a sectoral farm policy.

Third, enhanced agricultural growth and efficiency can make an important contribution to our national economy. Our superior ability to produce high quality food and fiber at competitive prices can enable American agriculture to increase its penetration of world markets and further reduce our overall trade eficit—provided that policies that promote other objectives do not unintentionally impede agricultural competitiveness.

Fourth, to foster efficiency and competitiveness, more rapid and flexible adjustment to shifting market demands is essential. Policies that seek to mask market signals and ward off inevitable changes only squander precious national resources. All current policies that make agriculture more rigid must be revised or discarded. All new proposals must be measured against the criteria of growth, efficiency, and adjustment.

Finally, agricultural policy must recognize the influence of history and the requirements of equity. Over the past 50 years, existing farm programs have become an integral part of the farm economy and rural way of life. To the extent that these policies are changed, the public as a whole has a responsibility to ease the burdens of the adjustment that will inevitably ensue.

Description of the Mixed Reform Policy

The mixed reform policy has four major elements: changing the economic environment for farmers while easing adjustment; enhancing stability; promoting conservation; and strengthening trade and foreign agricultural development. The following is a description of the specific programs that would be required.

Change and Adjustment

1. Income Support

The familiar target price/deficiency payments program would be continued. However, it would be reoriented toward smaller commercial farms (those that depend on farming for most of their family income and have farm product gross sales of no more than $200,000). It would not be designed to keep marginal farms in business indefinitely. Rather, it would be intended to ease adjustment over the next several years to more profitably sized operations, to less burdensome financial arrangements, or to new occupations.

Target prices would be gradually reduced, by five percent in each of the four years (Table 1). No limit on payments is included because eligibility would be limited to smaller commercial farms, which are unlikely to receive as much as $50,000 (the current limit) in any one year.

Table 1.
Mixed Reform Policy: Commodity Target Prices

Commodity	1985	1986	1987	1988	1989
Corn	3.03	2.88	2.74	2.60	2.47
Sorghum	2.88	2.74	2.60	2.47	2.35
Barley	2.60	2.47	2.35	2.23	2.12
Oats	1.60	1.52	1.44	1.37	1.30
Wheat	4.38	4.16	3.95	3.76	3.57
Rice	11.90	11.30	10.74	10.20	9.69
Soybeans	—	—	—	—	—
Cotton	81.0	77.0	73.1	69.4	65.9

Note: Prices are dollars per bushel except rice (dollars per cwt) and cotton (cents per pound).

2. Price Support/Loan Program

The price support loan program would also continue, but as a transition program to be phased out eventually. All farmers would be eligible for the program, with no limit on amounts loaned. To ease the adjustment inherent in greater reliance on the market, loan rates would be lowered only gradually, by five percent per year, to take into account both current farm economic conditions and the requirements of export competitiveness. The loan rates assumed in this analysis are shown in Table 1.

Table 2.
Mixed Reform Policy: Commodity Loan Rates

Commodity	1985	1986	1987	1988	1989
Corn	2.55	2.42	2.30	2.19	2.08
Sorghum	2.42	2.30	2.18	2.07	1.97
Barley	2.08	1.98	1.88	1.78	1.69
Oats	1.31	1.24	1.18	1.12	1.07
Wheat	3.30	3.14	2.98	2.83	2.69
Rice	8.00	7.60	7.22	6.86	6.52
Soybeans	5.02	4.77	4.53	4.30	4.09
Cotton	57.0	54.4	51.7	49.1	46.7

Note: Prices are dollars per bushel except rice (dollars per cwt) and cotton (cents per pound).

3. Production Control

Authority for temporary production control would be continued. The program would employ paid diversion rather than voluntary set-asides, and all farmers would be eligible.

Land would be enrolled on a bid basis for up to three years. Farmers would bid to idle land of proven productivity (e.g., $190 for an acre with a proven corn average yield of 100 bushels). The lowest bids would be accepted until the desired amount of land is removed from production.

Stability

Government reserve programs rest on the premise that individual actors in the private sector lack adequate incentives to hold socially desirable levels of commodities in reserve. In the most general terms, this proposition is widely accepted. But there is far less agreement about specific social objectives the reserves are to serve—and therefore, about precise reserve levels. As a result, current policy has provided government incentives for greater stockholding without quantifying needed or desired amounts.

Many experts believe that the reserve system in place since 1977 has failed to achieve either of its major stated objectives.

First, it has not worked very well to stabilize prices. There is no evidence that price fluctuations since the program was instituted have appreciably diminished. Second, it has not significantly increased total reserves. For the most part, public holdings simply displaced private holdings, at considerable cost to the taxpayer.

The mixed reform approach would include a national commodity inventory which would eventually replace current reserve programs. It would be designed to achieve two clearly defined stabilization goals: to provide buffer stocks that would temper abnormally high prices in times of short supply; and to ensure that, as a major commodity supplier to world food markets, we would be able to meet market demand in all but the most extreme situations.

This reserve policy would aim to maximize administrative simplicity while minimizing taxpayer costs and market distortions. The inventories would be farmer-owned, with a storage subsidy reflecting the social benefits of holding more stocks than would be accumulated without public incentives. Grain would enter the reserve for up to three years at the regular loan rate. The storage subsidy would be determined by farmer bid, with the lowest bids accepted until the desired quantity is obtained. No release or trigger prices are specified. The grain could be sold at the farmer's discretion, but the storage subsidy would cease upon sale.

It is neither practical nor economically feasible to carry stocks sufficiently large for all eventualities, however remote. Some judgment must be made

118

as to the level of stocks that can be supported. For our purposes, we assume that the national commodity inventory would contain a maximum of 10 percent of combined annual and export use for feed grains, and 20 percent for food grains.

Land Conservation

This approach would include a long-term conservation reserve that would be designed to shift the most highly erosive cropland to less intensive uses and bring about a better balance between long-term production and conservation.

The essential features of this reserve are as follows:

- The most highly erosive cropland would be identified by technicians using established soil and land use classification systems.
- A maximum amount of land to be enrolled in the program would be determined. Recent studies suggest that a level of 30 million acres would be enough to encompass most of the land at risk.
- A contract period of 10 years would be established during which eligible land would be enrolled in the reserve. For the duration of this period, specific restrictions would govern the enrolled land. Allowable uses and necessary conservation practices would be specified, including types of cover crops and provisions governing haying and grazing. Contract provisions might well build on existing land use conservation plans. Annual payments to farmers would be contingent on the fulfillment of their contractual obligations. In addition, "sodbuster" provisions would discourage the return of this land to cropping at the end of the contract period by permanently denying commodity program benefits on this acreage.
- Farmers owning this highly erosive land would offer the government a bid stating the annual amount they would require to shift this land to approved uses for 10 years. This bid could take one of two forms. It could cover both the annual rental payment and the government's share of the cost of conservation practices to be implemented in the first year. Alternatively, cost-sharing amounts could be administratively established by the government and excluded from the bid procedures.
- The bids would be arrayed and the lowest bids accepted until the desired or feasible amount of land was accepted, up to 30 million acres. The cost to the government would include the annual payment for the land plus the amount of the first-year cost-sharing for implementing practices to reduce erosion. We assume that these costs would average $50 per acre over the life of the contracts.

119

The 30 million acres would be distributed across commodities as follows:

	Percent	Million Acres
Wheat	58	17.4
Feed Grains	35	10.5
Cotton	7	2.1
TOTAL	100	30.0

The International Role of American Agriculture

1. Trade

At present, USDA operates several programs designed to expand exports. The most important are those offering concessional financing of one form or another to foreign purchasers of our farm products. They include the GSM-102 and GSM-5 programs, which offer both Commodity Credit Corporation guarantees of commercial loans at market interest rates and short and intermediate-term credit at below-market interest rates. In recent years, these have sometimes been combined to create "blended credit" financing packages.

The mixed reform approach would combine these programs into a single entity, a trade facilitation facility with common criteria and unified administration. It would focus on making credit available to heavily debt-burdened developing countries, for whom concessional financing is essential to expanded trade (at least in the next few years). This assistance would be expanded from present levels (Table 3).

A critical factor in justifying such additional expenditures is their ultimate effect on export sales. The principal determinant is what experts call "additionality"—that is, the amount by which export sales increase over what they would have been in the absence of such expenditures. The evidence on this point is unclear. For the purposes of this analysis, we make what we regard as a conservative assumption that additional guarantees of $700 million would expand exports by about five mmt annually.

Table 3.
Export Credit Programs

Fiscal Year	:	Credit Guarantees : GSM-102	:	Direct Loans GSM-5	:	TOTAL
			- - - million dollars - - -			
1982		1,368.5		46.9		1,368.5
1983		4,669.0		325.0		4,715.9
1984		4,179.5				4,504.5
1985		5,000.0*				5,000.0

Note: Program level. Guarantees actually made may be less.
Source: USDA.

2. Development

The PL 480 programs are a key to encouraging greater development of foreign agriculture. We recognize that these programs are by their very nature political and bound up with the broader aims of our foreign policy. Nevertheless, their effectiveness in encouraging agricultural development could be increased.

Thus, the mixed reform approach would refocus PL 480 more narrowly on agricultural development. Initially, total funding would not be increased from the $1.9 billion in FY 1985, but could be raised in future years if the programs prove their effectiveness in promoting growth of markets for U.S. agricultural products (Table 4).

Table 4.
PL 480 Expenditures — Titles I and II

Fiscal Year	:	Total Program Level	:	Net Expenditures	:	Total Metric Tons Grain Equivalent
		- - - millions - - -				- - - thousands - - -
1982		1,347		1,263		5,779
1983		1,400		992		5,991
1984		1,459		1,197		6,395
1985		1,906		1,560		7,521

Source: USDA and Commodity Credit Corporation.

3. Humanitarian Assistance

This policy would make few changes in current programs of international emergency assistance. The base funding of $650 million would be maintained, and supplemented in times of exceptional distress, such as the current African crisis.

Performance of Agriculture under the Mixed Reform Approach

Overall Performance

The mixed reform approach fashions a set of programs that appear relatively familiar yet represent a transition to greater reliance on the market. They are intended both to ease the burden of adjustment and to reduce contradictions among existing programs. The mixed reform strategy would therefore begin by effecting only modest changes in the performance of agriculture, but over time its impact would become more pronounced.

Production

The program would begin in 1986 with excessively large stocks on hand, especially those accumulated by the CCC. During 1986, some of those stocks would be returned to the market to bring holdings to more acceptable levels. This, along with implementation of the conservation reserve, would lead to a decline in planted acreage in the first year (Table 5). Plantings would expand in the subsequent years, averaging almost 279 million acres over the period. This amount is, however, below plantings in three of the past four years.

The 30 million acre long-term conservation reserve would quickly absorb much of the current slack in the system. This reserve should obviate the need for additional land diversion, although diversion authority would be continued to guard against successive years of abnormally favorable weather that could make further adjustment necessary.

Table 5.
Table 5.
Mixed Reform Policy: Program Crop Acreage and Production

Item	1982	1983	1984	1985	1986	1987	1988	1989
				- - - million acres - - -				
Area Planted	295.7	248.3	284.5	280.3	270.8	278.9	282.5	282.8
Area Idled	10.7	75.6	29.9	25.9	30.0	30.0	30.0	30.0
TOTAL (Base Acreage)	306.4	323.9	314.4	306.2	300.8	308.9	312.5	312.8
				- - - percent - - -				
Percent Idled	3.5	23.3	9.5	8.5	10.0	9.7	9.6	9.6
				- - - million tons - - -				
Production	395.2	253.3	364.5	370.6	364.2	380.0	394.5	402.0
				- - - tons - - -				
Production/Acre	1.34	1.02	1.28	1.32	1.34	1.36	1.40	1.42

Reflecting smaller plantings, production would decline slightly in the first year. Over the full four-year period, however, it would increase a total of almost 31 mmt—an average of 2.1 percent annually. Yields would continue their upward trend, reflecting long-term productivity growth.

Domestic and Export Use

Domestic use would expand slightly in the first year and then more rapidly in subsequent years (Table 6). It would average 243.2 mmt over the four years, growing over one percent annually. Exports, however, would grow 4.9 percent annually, reaching 155 mmt at the end of the period. (This growth rate reflects the increase of five mmt annually resulting from the expansion of export credit guarantees.) Combined use would expand by almost 40 mmt, slightly faster than the growth in production.

Over the four years, exports would account for an average of 37 percent of total use, and the value of export sales would expand by almost $6 billion. That expansion would be quite varied across different commodities, with very rapid growth for cotton and none at all for rice (Table 7).

Table 6.

Mixed Reform Policy: Program Crop Domestic and Export Use

Item	1982	1983	1984	1985	1986	1987	1988	1989
				- - - million tons - - -				
Domestic Use	229.2	208.9	218.6	233.7	236.6	243.2	246.2	246.6
Exports	124.0	118.9	132.5	128.0	136.7	141.3	148.4	155.2
TOTAL	353.2	327.8	351.1	361.7	373.3	384.5	394.6	401.8
Export Value* (billion dollars)					18.9	20.6	21.8	23.6	24.8

*Valued at the farm level price.

Table 7. Mixed Reform Policy: Program Crop Exports

Commodity	1984-85 Average	1986	1987	1988	1989	1986-89 Average	Percent Change
			- - - million tons - - -				
Corn	51.7	54.7	55.3	56.5	57.7	56.1	8.5
Wheat	41.7	45.2	46.6	49.3	52.0	48.3	15.8
Rice	2.9	3.2	3.2	3.4	3.5	3.3	13.8
Soybeans	20.8	22.9	25.1	27.5	29.5	26.3	26.4
Cotton	1.4	1.5	1.5	1.6	1.7	1.6	14.3

Stocks

At the beginning of the new programs in 1986, stocks will have reached almost 105 mmt (Table 8). Stocks would be drawn down in the first year to avoid depressing the market over the long term and to bring holdings to desired levels. The national inventory reserve would be filled at 37.3 mmt, reflecting the levels of feed and food grains specified in the program. Stocks would decline subsequently, averaging 24 percent of combined domestic and export use, compared to almost 29 percent in 1985.

Table 8.
Mixed Reform Policy: Ending Year Commodity Stocks

Commodity	1982	1983	1984	1985	1986	1987	1988	1989
Grains	142.0	73.9	85.6	95.0	86.3	82.0	83.5	84.2
Soybeans	9.4	4.8	6.8	8.5	8.3	7.9	6.4	5.8
Cotton	1.7	0.7	1.0	1.0	1.0	1.0	0.9	0.7
TOTAL	153.1	79.4	93.4	104.5	95.6	90.9	90.8	90.7
Reserve	76.4	31.9	35.2	40.2	37.3	38.2	39.2	40.0
CCC	40.5	13.8	19.6	22.3	18.0	18.0	18.0	18.0
Free	36.2	33.7	38.6	42.0	40.3	34.7	33.6	32.7
TOTAL	153.1	79.4	93.4	104.5	95.6	90.9	90.8	90.7
As Percent of Domestic and Export Use	43.3	24.2	26.6	28.9	25.6	23.6	23.0	22.6

Prices

The combination of the conservation reserve and somewhat greater exports would strengthen commodity prices, but the increases would not be large (Table 9). Overall, production would slightly outpace domestic and export use, inhibiting any significant upward movement.

Table 9. Public Interest Policy: Program Commodity Prices

Commodity	1982	1983	1984	1985	1986	1987	1988	1989
Corn	2.68	3.20	2.68	2.67	2.73	2.78	2.73	2.71
Sorghum	2.52	2.75	2.45	2.42	2.35	2.42	2.54	2.58
Barley	2.23	2.50	2.35	2.38	2.32	2.31	2.31	2.33
Rye	2.41	2.40	2.10	2.30	2.35	2.37	2.40	2.38
Oats	1.48	1.69	1.72	1.74	1.78	1.80	1.80	1.79
Wheat	3.55	3.54	3.42	3.45	3.47	3.55	3.55	3.52
Rice	8.11	8.79	8.30	8.20	9.10	9.10	9.00	8.60
Soybeans	5.69	7.75	6.20	6.00	6.30	6.35	6.80	6.90
Cotton	59.4	66.4	65.0	67.0	65.0	65.0	70.0	71.0

Note: Prices are dollars per bushel except rice (dollars per cwt) and cotton (cents per pound).

Income

Slightly stronger prices, coupled with gradual increases in volume, would increase the value of commodity sales over the next four years (Table 10.) Overall, the value of sales would grow over three percent per year, expanding almost 13 percent for the period. The average for the four years would be about 12 percent above the average for the previous period. Net farm income would average $25.3 billion, up about 9 percent over the previous four-year average.

Table 10
Mixed Reform Policy:
Value of Program Commodity Sales/Net Farm Income

Item	1982	1983	1984	1985	1986	1987	1988	1989
	- - - billion dollars- - -							
Value of Sales	50.5	48.2	50.0	49.9	51.9	54.4	57.5	58.6
Net Farm Income	22.3	16.1	31.0	22.5	24.0	25.4	25.7	26.2

This pattern would be balanced across the agricultural sector. Restrained growth in feed prices would benefit livestock producers, whose income would grow as well. Payments from government programs would decline. Overall, net farm income would be slightly higher than under current policy, and a greater share would stem from the market rather than the public sector.

Program Costs

The gradual reduction in government programs, at a pace designed to ease the burdens of transition and adjustment, would hold public costs relatively high in the first year. Later, substantial reductions would occur (Table 11). By 1989, costs would fall to about one-half the level of 1986. Over the four years, costs would average $2.8 billion annually, compared to $4.2 billion under the 1981 Act (not including the cost of the PIK program).

Table 11
Mixed Reform Policy: Program Cost Summary

Item	1982	1983	1984	1985	1986	1987	1988	1989
				- - - million dollars - - -				
Deficiency Payments	1,516.4	2,426.3	3,376.9	3,998.0	2,202.1	1,018.6	404.3	167.0
Storage	703.1	929.2	354.8	410.0	381.0	391.0	401.0	409.0
Land Diversion	72.0	900.4	677.7	742.0	0.0	0.0	0.0	0.0
LTCR	0.0	0.0	0.0	0.0	1,500.0	1,500	1,500	1,500
TOTAL	2,291.5	4,255.9	4,409.4	5,150.0	4,083.1	2,909.6	2,305.3	2,076

Reflecting both lower target prices and strengthening market prices, direct payments would decline steadily, averaging $0.9 billion annually (about one-third the average under the 1981 Act) and would be directed entirely to smaller commercial farmers. Storage costs for the national inventory reserve would rise slightly as the inventory gradually grows to keep pace with expanding domestic and export use. The average annual cost of $396 million for storage would be one-third less than the average of the previous four years. The conservation reserve would cost $1.5 billion per year, considerably more than land diversion under the 1981 Act, but less than half as much when the PIK program is taken into account.

Food Prices

This policy approach would not only be less expensive for taxpayers, but also reasonably advantageous for consumers in the long run. The slight strengthening of crop prices would put some upward pressure on food prices, but this would be partially offset by expanding production in the livestock sector. Over the long run, the more efficient use of resources and technology could lead to further declines in food prices.

Evaluation

Overall Effects

This mixed reform approach attempts to bring greater coherence to various important national objectives and to remove the more onerous features of present policy in a manner that is minimally disruptive of the farm sector and the national economy. It would not precipitate any radical changes in the short run, allowing adjustment to occur gradually. It would not raise farm income as rapidly as do some approaches. Nor would it reduce Treasury costs as rapidly. But it would point toward an improved balance between these (and other) objectives.

Food Safety, Quality, and Prices

This approach likely would have little tangible impact on the trends in food safety and quality. Over the long run, this approach would also be consistent with reasonable consumer food prices. Slight increases in prices for some commodities would be largely offset by declines for others during the transition period while resource adjustments are occurring. Some slight increase in food prices could occur as commodity prices strengthen and recovery commences in the farm sector.

Over the longer run, consumers could expect to benefit from this approach through gains from more efficient allocation of resources and continued application of new technologies. Reductions in government price support programs would point in the same direction.

Resource Conservation

This approach deals with agricultural resource concerns in two ways. First, it explicitly addresses the soil erosion problem by establishing a new long-term conservation reserve to shift the most highly erosive cropland into less intensive, more sustainable uses and by redirecting existing conservation programs to the most serious problems. Second, it would create a policy environment that removes perverse incentives to use land in ways inconsistent with conservation. With the phase-out of the commodity programs, promotion of surplus production from unsuitable lands would be greatly reduced, if not altogether eliminated.

While the long-term reserve would take erosion-prone acreage out of production, tough "sodbuster" restrictions would prevent the cultivation of additional unsuitable lands. This land would not simply be idled or irretrievably lost to productive use. Most of it could be used for livestock or forest product production. Moreover, it would be available for crop production in the event of critical national need.

This approach would also have positive effects for water use and conservation. It would eliminate incentives to squander scarce water supplies in the production of surplus commodities. And it would no longer encourage irrigation of crops in areas where production would be uneconomic without price supports.

Overall, this approach would be consistent with the wise use and conservation of the nation's agricultural natural resources.

128

Farm Income and Structure

1. Farm Income

The mixed reform approach would slow the decline in returns on agricultural investment. Gradual reduction of supports, establishment of the conservation reserve, and the targeting of supports to smaller farms would allow needed adjustment to the excesses of the 1970s to occur as nondisruptively as possible. In addition, it would permit the relatively smooth disentangling of government programs from the agricultural economy.

In the short term, net farm income would be higher than under current policy. In the longer run, returns would be less influenced by government interventions and more determined by the market. In a competitive environment with relatively free capital mobility, long term returns on farm investment would be close to returns on capital in other sectors of the economy.

2. Farm Structure

This approach addresses the structure of the farm sector in two ways. In the short run (the transition phase), it would direct income transfers to the smaller commercial farms—those depending primarily on farming for family income and having gross sales of no more than $200,000. This would give these farms a breathing-space to strengthen their financial position, enabling a greater number to survive and slowing concentration of production. Moreover, this approach would provide family-size commercial farms with a gradual (rather than abrupt) decrease in their dependency on government programs.

At the same time, the gradual phase-out of government programs would not indefinitely postpone structural adjustments. Continuous technological advances will ultimately compel small farms to expand, consolidate, or accept lower returns. Over the longer run, then, the mixed reform approach would permit farm structure to be determined primarily by market and technology rather than by government policies.

Economic Growth and Competitiveness

1. Stability

In the short run, during the transition period, the national inventory stock would provide a cushion against short supplies and rapid price increases. Gradually decreasing price and income programs would continue to protect farmers against collapsing prices. Over the next few years, the mixed reform approach would at worst be no less effective than current policy in promoting stability.

Over the longer run, this approach might actually be more conducive to stability than is current policy. It would not absolutely preclude recurring boom-bust cycles. Consecutive years of global production shortfalls could again cause rising prices and lead to over-optimistic expectations and rising asset values as occurred in the 1970s. However, the mixed reform approach would not inadvertently promote such swings. In fact, it would work to prevent them. It would not mask market signals and allow the accumulation of huge surplus stocks that depress prices and exacerbate downside swings. Farmers would reduce production in response to falling prices, dampening the depth and severity of the downturn. Conversely, farmers would expand production in times of rising prices. Adjustments would occur incrementally, substantially blunting upside and downside spikes.

Overall, the mixed reform approach is at least consistent with the goal of enhancing agricultural stability.

2. Exports

The mixed reform approach would reduce many current impediments to American agriculture's competitiveness in world markets. Reductions in price support loans would bring down commodity prices in the short run and send a clear signal to purchasers and competitors that we would no longer attempt to maintain a floor for those prices. Reduced use of production controls would point in the same direction. While placing substantial acreage in the conservation reserve would tend to raise prices, it would be a one-time adjustment intended to bring better balance between supply and demand and lead in the longer term to greater reliance on market forces. Retaining target price deficiency payments for smaller producers would stimulate some greater production, but the gradual lowering of target prices to levels much closer to market prices would virtually eliminate this distortion. Overall, this approach would help domestic agriculture to compete in the world.

Along with appreciation in the value of the dollar, the difficulty encountered by many developing countries in servicing the huge debt accumulated in the 1970s has been a major contributor to the four-year decline in export sales and loss of markets. Resolution of debt problems could increase the potential expansion of U.S. farm exports by as much as 20 percent, but at best this will take years. In the meantime, lifting trade with these countries from present low levels can occur only if foreign exchange and debt constraints are taken into account.

The mixed reform approach would recognize this by expanding financing assistance to these countries for purchases of our products. Instead of paying farmers not to produce, this approach would help them capture and hold markets while positioning themselves for longer-term market expansion and benefits.

130

Overall, this approach could expand U.S. exports in the short and intermediate-run and help build a more open regime of international trade.

International Responsibilities

This approach would help focus PL 480 activities on development assistance rather than surplus disposal, and it would modestly hasten indigenous agricultural development. Existing pressures on PL 480 funding could be eased by reductions in spending for domestic commodity programs. These steps would provide both an immediate boost to exports and a stronger foundation for longer-term trade growth and greater availability of food worldwide.

While strengthening our leadership in trade and development, this approach would continue our humanitarian assistance. Spending for this purpose could remain near present amounts, and adequate reserves coupled with relatively stable prices would allow us to respond flexibly and generously to emergencies.

SELECTED REFERENCES

Todd E. Petzel, "Moving Toward a Market Orientation: The Dilemma Facing Farm Policy in the 1980s." Coffee, Sugar, and Cocoa Exchange, New York, January 10, 1984.

Matthew D. Shane and David Stallings, *Financial Constraints to Trade and Growth: The World Debt Crisis and Its Aftermath*. FAER-211, Economic Research Service, USDA, December 1984.

Chapter 10

Comparing Approaches to the Farm Bill

Introduction

In a large, diverse nation—such as the United States—with a pluralistic political system, public policy almost always involves choices (or tradeoffs) among various objectives, not all of which can be maximized simultaneously. In this process, there are usually winners and losers, with the gains of some groups coming at the expense of others. It is rare indeed when a course of action will make everyone better off. This study rests on the premise that debate about the 1985 farm bill should be informed by a more systematic consideration of goals, a broader survey of policy options, a more realistic assessments of tradeoffs, a more explicit identification of winners and losers, and a more rigorous projection of the magnitude of gains, losses, and indirect effects of policy, than has been the case for many decades.

We began this study by reviewing the origin and evolution of agricultural policy and reexamining the purposes it might serve. Next, we surveyed the most widely discussed policy approaches, specified them in greater detail, and projected the economic and social consequences of each. In this chapter, we compare the performance of these policies and evaluate them in light of their impact on differing interests and goals.

Production

The four approaches—continuation of current policy (CCP), the free market (FM), restricted production (RP), and mixed reform (MR)—differ sharply in their impact on the use of the nation's cropland. Under the RP approach, plantings would be about 27 percent less than under the other three options (Table 1).

Table 1.
Comparison of Policy Options:
Area Planted

Options	1985	1986	1987	1988	1989	1986-89 Average
			— — million acres — — —			
CCP	280.3	278.8	280.1	276.7	281.7	279.3
FM	—	274.8	281.4	283.6	290.1	282.5
RP	—	209.5	206.4	201.4	198.2	203.9
MR	—	270.8	278.9	282.5	282.8	278.8

Conversely, RP would idle by far the most acreage (Table 2). It would withhold an average of some 109 million acres from production, while FM would withhold the least (7.5 million). Under MR, 30 million acres would be held in a long-term conservation reserve that would allow its continued use for agriculture (grazing and hay). CCP would idle 29 million acres, but with only minimal conservation practices and without attempting to identify the most highly erosive land.

Table 2.
Comparison of Policy Options:
Area Idled

Options	1985	1986	1987	1988	1989	1986-89 Average
			— — — million acres — — —			
CCP	25.9	26.1	27.6	30.7	29.7	28.5
FM	—	16.2	9.6	4.2	0.0	7.5
RP	—	103.1	106.2	111.2	114.4	108.7
MR	—	30.0	30.0	30.0	30.0	30.0

Given the moderate expansion projected for domestic and export use over the next four years, reaching a sustainable balance between production and demand requires reducing planted acreage by roughly 10 percent (Table 3). The four approaches handle this problem of excess capacity quite differently. Two, CCP and RP, simply postpone the question by temporarily withholding land from production, the former at taxpayer expense, the latter at the expense of consumers. They do not attempt to effect any longer-term adjustment that would bring total agricultural acreage into line with demand.

134

The other two approaches do offer some more permanent adjustment. FM would furnish a brief, three-year transition and then leave the matter to market forces. MR would provide a longer-term and less burdensome transition for farmers by dealing simultaneously with land allocation and soil erosion.

Table 3.
Comparison of Policy Options:
Percentage of Base Idled

Options	:	1985	:	1986	:	1987	:	1988	:	1989	:	1986-89 Average
						— — — percent — — —						
CCP		8.5		8.5		9.0		10.0		9.5		9.3
FM		—		5.6		3.3		1.5		0.0		2.6
RP		—		33.0		34.0		35.6		36.6		34.8
MR		—		10.0		9.7		9.6		9.6		9.7

Total production under all approaches is sufficient to meet market needs. RP greatly influences the size of the market, however, because its high prices sharply reduce both exports and domestic use. Production under RP is about 24 percent less than under the other three approaches, indicating that it would entail a significant reduction in overall economic activity (Table 4).

Table 4.
Comparison of Policy Options:
Production

Options	1985	1986	1987	1988	1989	1986-89 Average
			— — — million tons — — —			
CCP	370.6	375.7	382.3	383.0	391.6	383.2
FM	—	368.6	386.1	396.2	408.5	389.9
RP	—	295.7	294.7	293.8	294.1	294.6
MR	—	364.2	380.0	394.5	402.0	385.2

Domestic and Export Use

Combined commodity use in all markets is similar for three of the approaches, but sharply less for RP. While domestic use is expected to grow only slowly under the most favorable circumstances, it is responsive to price. The higher prices of RP would curtail use and preclude significant growth over the next four years, although there would be longer-term adjustments to the higher prices and use would eventually expand (Table 5.) Average use would be highest under FM, and only two percent smaller under CCP and MR.

Table 5.
Comparison of Policy Options:
Domestic Use

Options	1985	1986	1987	1988	1989	1986-89 Average
			— — — million tons — — —			
CCP	233.7	237.0	243.4	246.5	246.8	243.4
FM	—	242.1	247.6	250.4	253.3	248.4
RP	—	210.9	209.9	208.7	207.6	209.3
MR	—	236.6	243.2	246.2	246.6	243.2

Export demand shows considerable divergence among the options (Table 6). Exports would contract quickly under RP because of higher prices. Exports would rise under MR because of the combination of lower prices and expanded export credit programs. Because of reduced price floors, FM would allow for greater exports than would CCP. The rate of expansion under both FM and MR would be about five percent annually, slightly faster than for CCP, but substantially below the rapid rate of the 1970s.

Table 6.
Comparison of Policy Options:
Exports

Options	:	1985	:	1986	:	1987	:	1988	:	1989	:	1986-89 Average
					— — — million tons — — —							
CCP		128.0		131.7		136.3		143.3		150.0		140.3
FM		—		134.6		140.4		149.8		157.1		145.5
RP		—		100.1		98.0		95.9		93.9		97.0
MR		—		136.7		141.3		148.4		155.2		145.4

When the value rather than volume of exports is considered, however, the four approaches would produce much more similar results (Table 7). The average annual value would be highest for MR because of fairly stable prices combined with expanded volume from credit promotion. Even with considerably reduced volume, the average value would be only slightly less for RP because prices are much higher. Because of falling commodity prices, the value of exports would be lowest under FM, even though volume is highest. Over a period longer than the four years considered here, the MR and FM approaches would generate more rapid growth in revenues than the other two approaches, as demand becomes more responsive to prices.

Table 7.
Comparison of Policy Options:
Value of Exports

Options	:	1985	:	1986	:	1987	:	1988	:	1989	:	1986-89 Average
					— — — billion dollars — — —							
CCP		18.9		19.4		20.1		22.2		23.3		21.3
FM		—		18.5		19.4		21.2		22.4		20.4
RP		—		21.8		22.2		22.6		23.1		22.4
MR		—		20.6		21.8		23.6		24.8		22.7

Combined domestic and export use would be greatest for FM, slightly lower for MR and CCP, but much lower under RP (Table 8).

137

Table 8.
Comparison of Policy Options:
Total Use

Options	:	1985	:	1986	:	1987	:	1988	:	1989	:	1986-89 Average
						— — — millions tons — — —						
CCP		361.7		368.7		379.7		389.8		396.8		383.8
FM		—		376.6		388.0		400.2		410.4		393.8
RP		—		311.0		307.9		304.6		301.5		306.3
MR		—		373.3		384.5		394.6		401.8		388.6

Stocks

Average stockholdings also vary considerably across the approaches. They would be highest under CCP because of programs that encourage production in excess of use and require the United States to bear most of the burden of global adjustment (Table 9). This would be reflected in a higher proportion of total stocks to use than for the other approaches (Table 10). Stocks would be lowest under RP, where production is more tightly controlled. (The ratio of stocks to use would not be out of line with the other approaches.) The FM and MR approaches, allowing freer adjustment of production and consumption, would result in similar stockholdings.

Table 9.
Comparison of Policy Options:
Ending Year Commodity Stocks

Options	:	1985	:	1986	:	1987	:	1988	:	1989	:	1986-89 Average
						— — — million tons — — —						
CCP		104.5		111.5		114.1		107.4		102.2		108.8
FM		—		96.5		94.7		90.7		88.8		92.7
RP		—		89.2		75.8		65.0		57.5		71.9
MR		—		95.6		90.9		90.8		90.7		92.0

Table 10.
Comparison of Policy Options:
Ending Year Commodity Stocks in Relation to
Domestic and Export Use

Options	1985	1986	1987	1988	1989	1986-89 Average
			— — — percent — — —			
CCP	28.9	30.2	30.0	27.5	25.7	28.4
FM	—	25.6	24.4	22.7	21.6	23.6
RP	—	28.7	24.6	21.3	19.1	23.4
MR	—	25.6	23.6	23.0	22.6	23.7

Prices

Commodity prices under the four options largely reflect differences in the type and extent of government intervention. Prices would be highest under RP, where they are administratively determined and supply conditions managed so as to achieve them (Table 11). Price targets would result in levels almost 59 percent above those under the other approaches.

Table 11.
Comparison of Policy Options:
Index of Commodity Prices

Options	1985	1986	1987	1988	1989	1986-89 Average
CCP	336	336	335	348	353	343
FM	—	311	315	318	321	316
RP	—	477	490	509	529	501
MR	—	345	351	357	358	353

Prices would be lowest by a considerable margin under FM, which provides the most rapid reduction in price supports. Even though price guarantees are low, a large number of producers would be able to produce enough to generate quantities that maintain downward pressure on prices.

Prices would be higher under CCP than for FM, largely because of supports and production controls. Even though production outpaces consumption, government efforts to keep stocks off the market would prop up prices.

Prices under MR would average less than under RP, but higher than under the other options, both because the conservation reserve would help promote longer-term supply-use balance and because exports would expand slightly in response to added export credit.

Incomes

During the next four years, the value of agricultural production would be highest under RP (Table 12), as would net income (Table 13). Crop farmers would reap the bulk of these benefits. Over the span of more than one generation, after higher returns were capitalized in increased land values, income and return to capital would not be appreciably different than under the other approaches.

Table 12.
Comparison of Policy Options:
Value of Production

Options	1985	1986	1987	1988	1989	1986-89 Average
			— — — billion dollars — — —			
CCP	49.9	51.8	53.4	55.3	56.9	54.4
FM	—	48.4	49.6	51.7	53.8	50.9
RP	—	53.7	60.5	61.8	63.7	59.9
MR	—	51.9	54.4	57.5	58.6	55.6

Table 13.
Comparison of Policy Options:
Net Farm Income

Options	1985	1986	1987	1988	1989	1986-89 Average
			— — — billion dollars — — —			
CCP	22.5	23.6	24.3	25.1	25.3	24.6
FM	—	20.6	18.5	18.0	17.0	18.5
RP	—	25.1	26.1	26.6	27.4	26.3
MR	—	24.0	25.4	25.7	26.2	25.3

Among the other three approaches, MR would produce the highest incomes while avoiding the artificial capitalization that would be caused by

RP. Incomes under CCP would not be far different, however, because of the impact of production controls and price supports. Incomes would be lowest under FM, which provides the least downside protection. But overall, the size of these differences is modest enough to raise questions about the efficiency of methods designed to prop up farm incomes. It appears that farm income increases from such approaches would be far less than the combined cost to taxpayers, domestic consumers, and foreign purchasers.

Program Costs

Differences in direct taxpayer costs among these four approaches are especially pronounced (Table 14). The least expensive approach is RP, where administrative controls would be used to shift costs from taxpayers to consumers. The cost of this approach would be less than one-twentieth that of CCP.

Table 14.
Comparison of Policy Options:
Program Costs

Options	1985	1986	1987	1988	1989	1986-89 Average
			— — million dollars — —			
CCP	5,150.0	5,424.4	5,541.5	5,375.8	5,133.2	5,368.7
FM	—	2,530.0	388.0	340.0	340.0	899.5
RP	—	359.0	278.0	199.0	146.0	245.5
MR	—	4,083.1	2,909.6	2,305.3	2,076.0	2,843.5

CCP would be by far the most expensive of the approaches, because of continued deficiency payments, paid diversion programs, and huge stocks. At the end of the four-year period, imbalances would remain as severe as ever and stocks as large, despite the large outlays that would be required over the life of the bill.

The FM approach would be only modestly more expensive than RP. The rapid dismantling of government programs would result in sharply declining costs. After the first year, essentially the only costs would be for reserve stocks.

MR would be the second most costly, averaging slightly more than half the cost of CCP. The costs are relatively greater in the early years and then decline, although less rapidly than for FM, because of the gradual reduction in supports. Beyond the four-year period, costs would decline further, to the levels necessary for the commodity inventory and the conservation reserve.

141

Food Prices

Changes in food prices and consumer expenditures would be closely related to the effects of the different policy approaches on commodity prices and on the volume of consumption. RP would increase food prices the most. The initial escalation in grain prices and subsequent increase in livestock prices would raise food prices significantly and move them to a permanently higher level.

FM, on the other hand, would actually reduce food prices and consumer expenditures. CCP would allow at most gradual increases in food prices as commodity prices slowly move up. Consumer costs under MR would fall between FM and CCP.

Evaluation Relative to Goals

Food Safety, Quality, and Prices

The objective of a safe, nutritious, and high quality food supply would not be directly affected by the four approaches developed here.

FM and MR would both promote "reasonable" food prices for consumers by reducing contradictions in current policy and removing impediments to the implementation of market efficiencies and productivity-enhancing technological changes.

CCP is also consistent with relatively stable food prices. RP, on the other hand, would increase them significantly in both the short and the long term.

Resource Conservation

The four approaches treat resource problems quite differently, both directly, through targeted programs, and indirectly, through overall economic conditions that affect resource use.

MR would directly address these problem with a conservation reserve that takes fragile lands out of production. Moreover, it would reduce or eliminate programs that indirectly encourage unwise resource use. By restricting production, RP would relieve pressures for cultivating unsuitable lands and would cause the removal from production of much of the fragile land now farmed. FM would not explicitly treat the problem of conservation, but it would reduce pressures on resources by eliminating program incentives to cultivate erosive land. CCP, by contrast, would neither address the problem directly nor improve the overall economic incentives that affect conservation.

Farm Income and Structure

1. Farm Income

In comparing the effect of the four approaches on farm income, we must distinguish between the short and long run. In the long run, returns on farm investments will roughly equal those available in the overall economy, regardless of the specific farm policy in place. Capital resources will flow in and out of the sector depending on earnings there relative to those available elsewhere.

In the short run, however, the differences among policies would be significant. Farm incomes would be highest under RP, lowest under FM, with MR and CCP in between. Of the two intermediate options, MR would derive a higher percentage of total farm income from market transactions than would CCP, and a lower percentage from government transfers.

2. Farm Structure

RP is the only approach that would attempt to freeze the present structure of agriculture. It would provide higher returns to the farm sector, easing financial stress, and it would halt if not reverse the slide in asset values for many farmers while providing large windfall gains to many others.

FM would be the least consistent with the preservation of family-size commercial farms, because the rapid dismantling of government price support and income transfer programs would only exacerbate the financial stress these farms are now experiencing. CCP would neither improve nor worsen the situation of family farmers, while attrition would continue over time. While MR would reduce government programs below current levels, it would target these programs to mid-size commercial farms, reduce the programs at a slower pace than under FM, and encourage the adjustment essential to longer-term vitality.

Economic Growth and Competitiveness

1. Stability

The contributions of the four approaches to long-term economic stability are mixed. RP would virtually preclude boom-bust cycles through its rigid programs and administered prices, but at a high cost to the overall agricultural sector as well as to consumers.

The other three approaches would not absolutely preclude boom-bust extremes. In fact, their reliance on world markets would leave agriculture vulnerable to unpredictable shifts in demand. But they would deal in different ways with the conditions that give rise to cyclical shifts. By impeding adjustment and diminishing export competitiveness in times of declining prices, CCP would exacerbate the downswings. And—as in the past—it might well encourage upswings to relieve the pressure of high program costs and overly large stocks. FM and MR would encourage adjustments on an annual, incremental basis, dampening sharp swings. Beyond this, MR would maintain a larger reserve stock than would FM, contributing to stability in the face of sustained bad weather and crop failures.

Overall, RP contributes to stability by removing agriculture from market fluctuations and risks. Among the other three approaches, which expose agriculture to world market conditions, MR would deal with instability more effectively than would the two alternatives.

2. Exports

The four approaches differ widely in their impact upon international trade. RP would significantly reduce the volume of agricultural exports by effectively pricing American products out of world markets. Nor is CCP, with its frozen price supports, very conducive to trade expansion. Both FM and MR do better in this regard. By removing price floors altogether, FM would allow our products to be fully competitive. MR moves in the same direction, but more slowly. However, it would provide greater financial assistance to potential foreign buyers whose income and access to credit are temporarily reduced.

International Responsibilities

None of the four approaches would significantly affect the level or effectiveness of current efforts to promote agricultural development and provide humanitarian asistance.

Under CCP, RP, and FM, policies would remain more oriented to the disposal of American surpluses than to the development of foreign production. MR might modestly reorient policies toward development. None of the policies would dramatically alter our responsiveness to international emergencies, although the higher commodity prices experienced under RP might marginally decrease our willingness to provide additional foodstuffs to severely distressed regions.

Evaluation Relative to Interests

Thus far we have evaluated the four approaches to agricultural policy in relation to the broad national goals discussed earlier in this study. There is, however, another way of evaluating them, by asking how they affect different interest groups within our society—in particular, farmers, providers of agricultural inputs (machinery, seed, fertilizer), agricultural exporters, nonfarm inhabitants of rural America, and nonrural Americans who experience the effects of agricultural programs primarily through consumer food prices and federal budgetary outlays.

To begin this evaluation, let us rank-order the effects of the different options on key variables of interest to the various groups. This ordering is based both on the quantitative analysis developed in Chapters 6 through 9 and on the meaning of specific goals. For example, the groups that care about farm income will prefer, ceteris paribus, the option that maximizes farm income. The groups that care about farm structure will prefer the option that is best for mid-sized family farmers. And so on. In the following tables, "1" means the best for this category, while "4" means the worst. Fractional numbers indicates ties. The results are summarized in Table 15.

Table 15.
Comparison of Policy Options:
Interest Group Variables

Option	Farm Income	Farm Structure	Stability	Production	Volume of Exports	Consumer Food Prices	Farm Program Costs
CCP	3	2.5	4	3	3	3	4
FM	4	4	3	1	1.5	1	2
RP	1	1	1	4	4	4	1
MR	2	2.5	2	2	1.5	2	3

Now let us look at the interests of specific groups.

Farmers will be most concerned with farm income, farm structure, and agricultural stability. (Of course, many farmers may object to the restrictions on individual freedom inherent in RP, as they have in the past. For others suffering intensifying economic woes, concerns about "government intrusion" tend to diminish.)

Table 16.
Comparison of Policy Options:
Farmers

Option	Farm Income	Farm Structure	Stability	Total	Rank
CCP	3	2.5	4	9.5	3
FM	4	4	3	11	4
RP	1	1	1	3	1
MR	2	2.5	2	6.5	2

Agricultural input providers will be most concerned about the overall level of farm production.

Table 17.
Comparison of Policy Options:
Input Providers

Option	Farm Production	Total	Rank
CCP	3	3	3
FM	1	1	1
RP	4	4	4
MR	2	2	2

Agricultural exporters will be most concerned about the volume of exports.

Table 18.
Comparison of Policy Options:
Exporters

Option Option	Volume of Exports	Total	Rank
CCP	3	3	3
FM	1.5	1.5	1.5
RP	4	4	4
MR	1.5	1.5	1.5

The interests of *nonfarm rural Americans* are more complex. These individuals are affected not only by the prosperity or suffering of farmers, but also by the level of economic activity in sectors that depend on farming. Thus, their wellbeing is a function of farm income, farm structure, agriculture stability, overall production, and volume of exports. (To a much more limited extent, they are also affected by food prices and taxation to pay for farm programs. But for the purposes of the current analysis, these effects can be ignored.)

Table 19.
Comparison of Policy Options:
Rural Americans

Option	Income	Structure	Stability	Production	Exports	Total	Rank
CCP	3	2.5	4	3	3	15.5	4
FM	4	4	3	1	1.5	13.5	3
RP	1	1	1	4	4	11	2
MR	2	2.5	2	2	1.5	10	1

Finally, *nonrural Americans* will be most affected by food prices and the costs of farm programs.

Table 20.
Comparison of Policy Options:
Costs for Nonrural Americans

Option	Food Cost Change (1985-89: $ billion)	Program Cost Change (1985-89: $ billion)	Total	Rank
CCP	0	0	0	3
FM	− 17	− 5	− 22	1
RP	+ 20	− 5	+ 15	4
MR	− 10	− 3	− 13	2

NOTE: Food Cost Change represents program effects only, exclusive of population effects and increases in costs of production.

Let us summarize the results of this analysis across the different interest groups.

Table 21.
Comparison of Policy Options for Groups

Option	Farmers	Input Providers	Exporters	Rural Americans	Nonrural Americans
CCP	3	3	3	4	3
FM	4	1	1.5	3	1
RP	1	4	4	2	4
MR	2	2	1.5	1	2

Three conclusions are suggested by this summary.

First, CCP fares rather badly in the interest-group evaluation. It is the first choice of no group, and the third or last choice of all groups.

Second, both FM and RP can be viewed as divisive policies. Each would be strongly favored by some groups and fervently resisted by others. In fact, they are virtually mirror-images of one another. RP would be praised by farmers and rural Americans and damned by everyone else, while FM would be unacceptable to the farm-rural coalition.

Third, MR can be viewed as the basis of possible compromise and consensus. It is the last choice of no group, and the first or second choice of all. In addition, it would have considerable appeal to strong partisans of conservation.

Conclusion:

Looking Toward The Year 2000

In Section III, we sought to provide the reader with a factual and analytical basis for evaluating different approaches to farm legislation in 1985. In this conclusion, we place this choice in a context somewhat broader than that usually governing legislative debates: the longterm interests of our country and of future generations.

As we look to the future, there appear to be three basic realities that will shape the environment of agricultural policy.

The first is technology. A recent report by the Congressional Office of Technology Assessment (OTA) examines the impact of expected technological developments on American agriculture. It identifies about 150 emerging technologies that could revolutionize agricultural production. Ranchers may be able to raise beef cattle much larger than those found today. Dairy farmers may be able to control the sex of calves and to increase milk production by more than 10 percent without increasing feed intake at all. Crops may be genetically altered to resist pests and disease, grow in extreme of climates and soils, and produce their own fertilizer. Modern information systems may provide the ability to monitor individual livestock and regulate feeding and breeding patterns accordingly. Although the timing and impact of specific innovations cannot be precisely identified, the aggregate effect of technology will be to accelerate the growth rate of agricultural productivity between now and the end of this century. And, as the OTA report shows, this enhanced productivity will only intensify the forces that are already squeezing mid-sized producers and generating a more concentrated, specialized, corporate agricultural sector.

The second basic reality is the enormous impact of macroeconomic policy on agriculture. As we showed earlier, agriculture is now one of the most credit-dependent, interest rate-sensitive sectors of our economy. Thus, the interaction between fiscal and monetary policy has a far greater impact on farm operations and income than does farm legislation. At present, it is impossible to predict whether current efforts to trim the federal budget deficit will succeed. But assuming that other conditions do not worsen significantly, the outcome of these efforts will have an important effect on agriculture. As Chapter 3 makes clear, reducing the deficit to 2 percent of GNP would mean a multi-billion dollar increase in annual farm income—anywhere from 25 to 60 percent. Farmers who cannot make a profit at current real interest rates would have a fighting chance to survive. Land values would tend to stabilize and pressures on rural communities and lending institutions would be reduced. On the other hand, the failure to reduce the budget deficit would virtually ensure the continuation of tight money and record real interest rates, which would in turn hasten the departure of tens, even hundreds of thousands of farmers from the agricultural sector.

The third basic reality is the integration of American agriculture into the world economy. The productive capacity of our agricultural sector far exceeds potential demand from our domestic market. If we want to improve the current supply-demand imbalance, which has produced lower commodity prices for farmers and higher program costs for taxpayers, we have only two choices. We can rigorously restrict production, a policy which (as we have seen) imposes large costs on important parts of the agricultural sector and the broader economy. Or we can try to restore sustained growth in exports, an approach that would require us to emphasize productivity and international competitiveness, to foster a more open and fair regime of international trade, to address severe currency distortions, and to give renewed attention to the longterm factors—including income and international debt in developing countries—that ultimately determine sustainable levels of demand for our agricultural products.

These three realities are not unique to agriculture. In fact, we are struck by the parallels between agriculture and other troubled areas of our economy. The impact of technological advances here and abroad, of skewed fiscal and monetary policies, and of restricted global markets for American products has staggered agriculture and manufacturing alike. (Unlike manufacturing, imports are not yet a serious problem for most key agricultural commodities, but there are indications that even this traditional advantage is giving way under the impact of the strong dollar.) In agriculture, as in manufacturing, fundamental and traumatic changes are inevitable even if macroeconomic policy is more effectively managed and other nations cooperate in removing barriers to trade. In agriculture, as in manufacturing, we have three basic choices: to surrender to change, to resist it, or to try to shape and manage an orderly, humane process of adjustment.

In agriculture, as in other areas of our economy, there are strong constituencies for options one and two. On the basis of the criteria developed in this report, we believe that serious consideration must also be given to the third option, adjustment, which attempts to balance the need for growth (and therefore the requirements of efficiency and competitiveness) with the proposition that growth is for human beings (and not the other way around).

150

Let us be clear that the path of adjustment will not be easy. The United States will have a steel industry in the 1990s, but it won't look much like the steel industry of the 1970s. Hundreds of thousands of unemployed steel-workers will have to be told that they will never regain their jobs. Most will need retraining; many will be forced to leave their communities to find new work. In the process, many cities and towns will be dealt a heavy blow.

Similar changes can be anticipated in agriculture. Barring drastic and unlikely changes in our agricultural policies, by the turn of the century there will be hundreds of thousands fewer farmers. The rate of attrition will be greatest among mid-sized family farms. The average farm will be much larger than it is today, and vertical integration of the production process will be far advanced. In the process, many rural communities will be hard-hit, and without alternatives, some will be turned into ghost towns.

This vision of the future implies the need for a much more farsighted approach to U.S. agricultural policy—an approach that is far more sensitive to the interests of future generations. In this connection, three broad considerations seem to us to be of particular importance.

First, it is clear that contemporary agricultural policies and programs can no longer be devised and implemented without regard to their potentially adverse effects on the country's natural resources and environment. It is no longer possible for policymakers to ignore the fact that government activities that significantly affect agricultural markets also influence the resource base and the environment, frequently for the worse.

Over the next decade, agricultural policy should come to reflect a more adequate awareness of resource and environmental problems, including soil and water conservation, groundwater and surface-water pollution (runoff from agricultural chemicals), salinization and compaction of croplands, and destruction of biological diversity through the destruction of wildlife habitat and species as well as through the shortsighted use of genetic engineering techniques. These problems are sufficiently serious and widespread to justify a reexamination of the government's historical reliance on voluntarism and economic incentives to cope with agricultural resource issues.

A second long-term policy concern is the legacy to rural communities of the concentration of ownership and control of agricultural resources, primarily of land. We have gone to some lengths to describe how drastically U.S. agriculture has changed over the past half century and to describe how those changes have rendered obsolete many aspects of America's agricultural policies. We have dwelt less on the difficult question of what becomes of the small towns and communities in the wake of a more or less inexorable evolution of U.S. agriculture toward fewer, larger farms. As we have shown, the traditional farm programs are no longer (if they ever were) very effective instruments for alleviating rural poverty, for maintaining a sectoral structure of medium-size family farm operations, or for assisting beginning farmers. Clearly, however, society is no more justified in ignoring rural than urban poverty, particularly when lack of sustainable employment is a key cause of poverty. The concentration of control over agriculture production and resources and restricted entry into agriculture raise much more difficult issues, but we are convinced that policymakers will find it harder and harder to avoid their implications for economic opportunity and for the quality of life in rural areas. We find it difficult to accept that it is in the best interests of the nation to allow the number of farms and the farm population to decline precipitously or indefinitely. No national agricultural policy can be considered comprehensive that does not adequately reflect the contribution that employment opportunities in agriculture and rural America can make to the overall level of opportunity and prosperity in our society.

A third policy challenge facing American agriculture is the role it can and should play in world affairs. Current policy is driven by levels of domestic production of major crops, which frequently exceed both domestic and foreign demand. The world economy of the 1980s and 1990s will not lend itself to government management of domestic production, in no small measure because of the impact of essentially unpredictable foreign government decisions and levels of foreign production on U.S. agricultural exports. Moreover, a thoroughly internationalized agricultural sector raises basic questions about the niche American agriculture should occupy in the country's foreign policy. For example, our ability to export will depend crucially on the growing well-being of the peoples in developing countries. This, in turn, may well require significant changes in current policies, ranging from conditions on repayment of Third World debt, to restrictions on the use of American aid, to protectionist barriers regulating the import of manufactured goods such as shoes and textiles into this country.

However difficult it is to see and draw inferences from the future, it is far easier to describe the outlines of a new approach to agricultural policy than it is to build an effective coalition for change. The making of public policy in this area (as in so many others) is subject to enormous constraints. The growing number of groups with a strong interest in agricultural policy fragments the system and pushes it toward stalemate, biasing the outcome in favor of a status quo that is widely judged to be unsatisfactory. Past policies, however misguided, have generated powerful client constituencies and have induced farmers, lenders, and many others to make personal or financial commitments that cannot be quickly reversed. Finally, record budget deficits severely constrain the amount of public resources that can be devoted to any agricultural policy, however widely supported and forward-looking.

As citizens and policy-makers examine the 1985 farm bill as a bridge to the next decade of agriculture, they are all too aware of these limits. It is easy to throw up one's hands in despair and to conclude that nothing much

152

can be changed. Key legislators have already opined that current policy will be continued, if only on an interim basis, not because the national interest would be thus served, but rather because the dead hand of past commitments is too heavy to lift.

This study of basic options for the next farm bill is intended as a counterweight to such forces. Crucial public choices should be made in light of the fullest possible public information about the consequences of different courses of action. Policy should be adopted by deliberation, not by default. It is our belief that this conception of effective democracy in action is not the naive residue of some civics text, but rather the most necessary and practical response to the many perplexities that beset the formulation of food and agriculture policy in this country.

Appendix A

Other Commodity Programs

Dairy

The dairy industry is one of agriculture's largest sectors. Wisconsin and California are the leading milk producing states, and together with Minnesota, New York, and Pennsylvania account for more than half of total production (Table 1).

Table 1.
Five Largest Milk Producing States

STATE	1984
	—percent of U.S. total—
Wisconsin	17.4
California	11.3
New York	8.4
Minnesota	7.6
Pennsylvania	7.0
TOTAL	51.6

Source: USDA

In recent years, the trend toward larger dairies has become increasingly important (Table 2). Large units are now dominant in the Southern Plains and Pacific regions, and they are rapidly gaining ground nationwide.

In 1978, 50 percent of the dairies had fewer than 20 cows, accounting for seven percent of total cows. By 1982, only 42 percent of the dairies had less than 20 cows, accounting for only five percent of the total. During this period, large dairies with more than 100 cows rose from five to seven percent of all dairies and from 31 to 36 percent of all cows.

Table 2.
Changes in Dairy Industry Structure

	:	Farms		:	Cows		:
Number of Cows	:	1978	: 1982	:	1978	: 1982	:
1 - 4		36	29		2	1	
5 - 19		14	13		5	4	
20 - 49		30	32		32	27	
50 - 99		15	19		30	32	
100 or more		5	7		31	36	
TOTAL		100	100		100	100	

Source: Census of Agriculture

Feed is the most important cost of milk production, accounting for 40 percent of total cash and capital replacement costs in 1984. Traditionally, milk production has been located where feed costs are lowest and forage is cheaply and readily available. On this basis, the Northeast, Lake States, and Corn Belt each developed large dairy industries.

Since World War II, this traditional structure has changed dramatically. Because of higher productivity, large operations are able to operate profitably in areas of relatively high feed costs. This has encouraged both the concentration of dairy production in larger operations and the geographical decentralization of production, which has spread to new states and regions.

Dairy product prices are regulated directly through three basic programs. First, they are supported through USDA purchases of butter, cheese, and nonfat dry milk (NDM) at prices designed to hold farm milk prices at designated levels. When supplies are excessive, USDA builds very large inventories that cannot be resold commercially in the United States except at sharply increased market prices. As a result, large amounts of CCC butter, cheese, and NDM are sold or donated for noncommercial uses.

In addition to the price supports that set a minimum national average price for manufacturing milk, federal market orders set minimum prices for milk for fluid use in 45 regional markets. In order to encourage local fluid milk production, the minimum price in each of the orders is based on distance from the region of greatest surplus production (Wisconsin). Market orders link regional prices directly to the average support price and are changed in tandem with the support price. About 80 percent of the fluid milk is sold under market orders.

The third major program restricts imports to prevent their interference with domestic price supports. Since 1974, imports of milk products have been held to between 1.5 and 2 percent of U.S. production, largely by quotas on imported cheeses.

CCC purchases of dairy products have often been large, exceeding four billion pounds in 19 of the 34 years of the program's history, but recent surpluses have been unprecedented (Table 3). In 1953/54, CCC bought 11.3 billion pounds (at a cost of less than $500 million), the greatest amount until 1981; since then purchases have averaged 13.4 billion pounds and the government inventory has grown in spite of programs to sell stocks overseas and donate them to needy people and institutions in the United States. At the beginning of FY 1985, the federal government had a dairy product inventory equivalent to 19 billion pounds of milk, valued at $3.7 billion.

Table 3.
Size and Cost of the Milk Price Support Program

Fiscal Years

Item	:	1979	:	1980	:	1981	:	1982	:	1983	:	1984 Estimate
						—billion pounds—						
CCC Purchases		1.1		8.3		12.5		13.8		16.6		10.4
Inventory		3.0		8.4		16.4		20.2		23.2		19.1
Cost (billion dollars)		—		1.0		1.9		2.2		2.5		1.5

Source: USDA.

For many years, milk price supports were tied to the "parity" formula, with the Secretary of Agriculture required to establish supports between 75 and 90 percent of parity. In 1977, Congress raised the minimum support price from 75 to 80 percent of parity and required twice yearly adjustments, provisions that were continued until 1981. Producers responded with enormous increases in output. As surpluses grew, government costs rose sharply.

Since 1980, several attempts have been made to reduce government program costs:

• In early 1981, legislation was passed to forego the last price support increase required by the 1977 bill.

• The 1981 Act no longer based supports directly on parity as previous laws had done, but it did specify minimum support prices that increased each year. While reestablishing 75 percent of parity as the nominal minimum, it authorized the lower supports when production was in surplus. The year the law was signed, net government purchases reached a record 12.5 billion pounds at a cost of $1.9 billion.

• The FY 1982 Budget Act eliminated the price support increase scheduled for October 1982 and authorized an assessment of up to $1.00 per cwt on all commercial sales.

In spite of these measures, milk production incentives continued to in-

157

crease through early 1983, long after markets had come under pressure. In a renewed effort to bring production into line with consumption, the 1983 Dairy and Tobacco Adjustment Act authorized cash payments to farmers who agreed to market less milk between January 1, 1984 and March 31, 1985 than they had during a 1981 base period. The payment rate was $10 per cwt reduction. In addition, the price support was reduced 50 cents, with authority for two other adjustments in 1985. Producers who participated in the program were free to comply with their agreement by reducing cow numbers or by changing rations and daily milking schedules but were required to produce between 5 and 30 percent less milk. Participation in the program was low (about 38,000 farmers) and participants agreed to cut production by only 7.5 billion pounds (5.4 percent of 1983 production).

For the industry, the diversion program together with the increase in production costs in late 1983 and 1984 stemming from drought and the PIK program was followed by large decreases in cow numbers, a downturn in production per cow, and 1.6 percent lower 1983/84 production. CCC net purchases declined to 9.8 billion pounds, and program costs declined to a net of $1.5 billion (including both diversion payment costs and returns from producer assessments).

Nevertheless, the 1983 Act does not appear to have improved long-term prospects for balanced supply and use. While cow numbers are reduced, production capacity continues to exceed expected levels of consumption. The factors that caused the FY 1984 production decline seem unlikely to be repeated.

Peanuts

The 1.5 million acres planted to peanuts constitute less than half of one percent of total U.S. crop acreage. Peanuts are grown on 28,000 farms, nearly 70 percent of which harvest less than 50 acres.

The peanut industry has been among the nation's most closely regulated since the 1930s, with production controlled by acreage allotments and domestic sales restricted by individual farm quotas. The marketing quota is distributed among producers in 16 states, heavily concentrated in seven southern states—Georgia, Alabama, North Carolina, Texas, Oklahoma, Virginia, and Florida. One-half of all quota production occurs under rented quotas with nearly ten percent under quotas rented separately from land.

Growing surpluses and rising program costs brought changes in the 1977 Act, the first since 1949. Production and sales controls were continued, but a two-price system was instituted. Supplies for the domestic market were tightly controlled with high price supports, but lower price supports for additional production permitted exports at competitive world prices.

The "Agriculture and Food Act of 1981" eliminated peanut acreage allotments but retained poundage quotas assigned to specific farms. Currently, any farmer can grow and market peanuts, but only production from quota farms can be used for domestic edible consumption and, therefore, qualify for the higher price support. The price support for quota peanuts was set at not less than $550 per ton for 1982—up from $455 per ton in 1981 and the $420 minimum prescribed in the 1977 Act. Annual increases in the quota support level were permited beginning in 1983 to reflect product cost increases (excluding land) with the increase limited to six percent.

The lower support price for "additional" peanuts (about one-third the rate for quota peanuts) was set at a level designed to avoid any net cost to the government. This rate is based on the demand for peanut oil and meal, expected prices for other vegetable oils and protein meals, and the demand for peanuts in foreign markets.

The 1981 Act also lowers the poundage quota by nearly 25 percent over the life of the bill, from 1.44 million tons in 1981 to 1.10 million tons in 1985.

Sugar

The U.S. sugar industry is relatively small, with 2,900 cane producers and 9,800 sugar beet producers. Sugarcane is grown in Florida, Hawaii, Louisiana, Texas, and Puerto Rico, while beets are grown in many states. Both cane and beet production depend on large, costly sugar factories which have been declining in numbers for many years. Sugar production has been trending downward slowly since 1970, except for an increase in the mid-1970s following the high sugar prices of 1974 and 1975. Since 1975, cane acreage has fallen one percent while beet acreage is 27 percent lower.

Between 1948 and 1974, U.S. sugar policy was embodied in a series of Acts which stabilized domestic prices through country-by-country import quotas. That law was allowed to expire in 1974, and a variety of programs have since been used. From 1974 to 1977, domestic prices followed world price movements very closely. With weakening prices, the Congress in 1977 mandated a two-year price support based on parity, achieved by fees and duties on imported sugar.

The 1981 Act uses price support loans and fees, duties, and quotas as necessary to prevent import interference with the price support program. In administering this program, CCC has maintained domestic market prices for raw sugar high enough to encourage the repayment of price support loans. A domestic price objective, the Market Stabilization Price (MSP), determines the required fees and duties or the quantities to be imported when quotas are in effect. Because the fees cannot exceed 50 percent of the world price and there is a maximum duty, the MSP cannot always be achieved by fees and duties alone when world prices fall to very low levels, as has been the case recently. With its import restrictions, the sugar program operates at low government costs because it manages the domestic supply and maintains prices at levels that prevent the forfeiture of sugar to the CCC. This strategy results in higher costs for sugar and sugar products than if the program depended on direct government payments. Consequently, it reduces consumption of sugar and other foods.

Tobacco

One million acres of tobacco are grown by 250,000 farmers, an average of four acres per farm. Acreage allotments and quotas give farmers the right to grow and market tobacco. Because the supply of these allotments and quotas is rigorously limited, they have a capitalized value of $7,500 to $8,500 per acre. They can be sold or rented, subject to certain restrictions. High allotment and quota rental rates (25 to 35 percent of production costs) also reflect the production control policies. Price supports are based on parity. If a lot of tobacco sold at auction fails to receive a bid of one cent per pound over the support price, it is bought under a CCC loan by a grower cooperative.

Appendix B

Quantitative Methodology for Evaluating Alternative Policy Proposals

An important part of the consideration and comparison of alternative policy proposals for the farm sector is the evaluation of how they might operate if implemented. To what extent will they achieve the objectives for which they were designed? What will be their impact on different groups? And what will they cost?

It is, of course, impossible to predict the performance of the agriculture sector very far into the future with any degree of reliability because of the strong influence of natural forces and the variability in foreign markets. But useful information can be obtained from projecting the most probable outcomes under alternative policies.

Conducting such an analysis involves several elements. First, the policy options must be specified with some precision. This requires detailed development of their provisions and decisions about how the programs would be operated under various situations. The programs allow for considerable administrative discretion, for example, in the timing and extent of acreage diversion for production control. The projection process thus requires some judgments about the likely discretionary behavior of the Secretary of Agriculture. (For a fuller discussion of this issue, see Appendix C.)

Next, the macroeconomic environment of agricultural policy must be specified. This involves both a domestic and an international element, now much more closely related than ever before. The international aspect—income growth of foreign consumers, population growth, and trading policies—is reflected in the demand for U.S. exports. Also, as has been vividly illustrated in recent years, that demand is indirectly affected by U.S. fiscal and monetary policies, which help determine the value of the dollar and the competitiveness of our products in foreign markets.

Assumptions about programs and macroeconomic variables are then integrated with historically-based economic relationships to predict levels of production, consumption, and trade. This in turn permits the determination of commodity prices, farm receipts, food prices, Treasury costs, and other

161

economic impacts on groups such as farmers, agribusinesses, consumers, and taxpayers.

The process begins with development of a benchmark or baseline, which typically assumes continuation of the current policy for another four years (in this case 1986-89). Projections are developed for annual production, consumption, trade, and stocks. The analysis focuses on the nine major crops covered by the programs: food grains (wheat and rice), feed grains (corn, sorghum, barley, oats, and rye), soybeans, and cotton.

The basic analytical construct is a commodity supply-use table (Table 1). The beginning point of the analysis is the 1986 crop year with stocks carried over from 1985. These stocks plus production in 1986 plus any imports will constitute the available supply. (Imports of the program crop commodities typically are very small, usually limited to the amounts of specific commodities needed to produce specialty goods.) Determining the quantity of each crop that will be produced involves projecting how farmers in the aggregate will respond to present and anticipated economic conditions such as commodity prices and production costs. This involves estimating the area to be planted, the area expected to be harvested (some acreage each year is lost to drought and flooding or used for purposes other than grains), and the expected yields. Average weather conditions are assumed to prevail, and yields are increased each year to reflect technological developments. The rate of annual increase is usually based on historical trend rates, adjusted to reflect any special conditions. (For example, when large diversion programs are used, national average yields may rise faster than normal because farmers typically increase their use of inputs on the land remaining in production.) Total production is simply the product of acreage under cultivation times yield.

Table 1.
llustrative Supply-Use Table

Item	:	1986	:	1987	:	1988	:	1989	:
Area Planted....................									
Harvested Area...................									
Area Idled......................									
Participation Rate................									
Yield..........................									
Supply									
Beginning Stocks................									
Imports									
Production......................									
Total Supply................									
Use									
Feed									
Food, Industrial & Seed									
Total Domestic Use									
Exports									
Total Use									
Ending Stocks									
Farmer-Owned Reserve									
CCC Inventory..................									
Free Stocks.....................									
Prices									
Season Average Price									
Regular Loan Rate................									
Reserve Loan Rate...............									
Deficiency Payment Rate...........									
Target Price									

Next, an estimate of total expected use is developed. Use is divided between the domestic market (for food, feed, seed, and industrial purposes) and the foreign market (exports). Domestic usage is relatively stable from year to year. It is largely determined by population and income growth, with some shifts among products in response to changing consumer tastes and preferences, dietary concerns, and new product development (such as corn sweeteners). Annual export demand is influenced by numerous factors, including price, the value of the dollar, the financial status of potential foreign buyers, and quantities to be shipped under concessional programs such as PL 480. The sum of domestic and export usage constitutes total use.

Finally, subtracting total usage from the available supply provides the estimate of total end-of-year stocks, which are carried into the next year. It is important to break down this total by estimating the quantities of carryover stocks in various positions. The market availability and price of stocks varies considerably, depending on whether they are held in the farmer-owned reserve or under CCC ownership (forfeited under the loan

163

program), both of which have specific release prices, or are held by the trade (the so-called "free stocks").

Construction of annual supply-use estimates is not simply the sequential process described above. Rather, it is really an iterative procedure. It involves the simultaneous determination of price and demand, while each in turn influences the other. Farmers base their planting decisions largely on expectations of the prices they can obtain several months hence when the product is to be sold. However, once plantings and carryover stocks are known, and barring adverse weather, reliable estimates of the supply available within the year are widely available to the market. Within a given year, it largely is the strength of market demand that determines the price. From these considerations, the season average price is estimated for the year.

The estimated price that results from the expected supply and demand conditions is then compared to the various program parameters to determine program cost. If the market price is below the target price, the amount of the deficiency payment per unit is then determined. This amount times the quantity of production eligible for payment provides estimates of the total direct program payments.

The determination of the quantity of production eligible for payment is a function of the extent of farmer participation in the program. Program provisions are announced well before the planting season so farmers can consider them in formulating their plans. If a voluntary diversion program of 10 percent is announced, then farmers must idle 10 percent of the base acreage of their commodity on their farm to be eligible for the commodity loan program and the deficiency payment. For example, about 60 percent of the wheat base acreage typically is enrolled in such programs. At times, paid diversion may be a part of the program as well. Farmers then may voluntarily idle another (say) 10 percent of their base acreage and receive a fixed payment per acre (usually offered as a price per bushel times the program yield established for that acreage). The program cost equals acres idled times the payment rate.

In addition to estimating the Treasury costs of the programs, these commodity price estimates are used to project farm receipts and consumer food prices. Farm receipts in turn provide the point of departure for estimating net farm income (Table 2).

Table 2
Illustrative Net Farm Income Table

1. Cash receipts from sale of commodities
2. Direct government payments
3. Other cash income
4. Non-money income
5. Gross income (1 + 2 + 3 + 4)
6. Inventory change
7. Adjusted gross income (5 + 6)
8. Production expenses
9. Net farm income (7 - 8)

This entire process is aided by computer models that incorporate equations with parameters derived from historical experience. These equations provide estimates of such key variables as consumption response to price changes, price response to changes in stocks, and farmers' planting response to price changes. But the estimation procedures cannot be simply self-contained and mechanical. Because of the complexities introduced by the discretionary administration of farm programs and other complicating factors, the empirical model estimates must be checked against—and sometimes adjusted by—the analyst's judgment.

The procedure just described is repeated for each of the four years 1986-89. From this four-year review, assessments can be made of the likely economic state of agriculture as well as of the efficacy of the programs and their consequences for other groups affected by agricultural policy.

This baseline or benchmark is used as the reference point for the assessment of alternative policies. Assumptions about the prevailing macroeconomic environment are held constant, as are assumptions about the weather. Within this analytical structure, changes in the economic performance of the agricultural sector are determined by the ways that different approaches would alter the behavior of both producers and consumers, including foreign consumers.

Appendix C

Administrative Discretion In Commodity Programs

Each farm bill contains myriad specific requirements about the operation of the commodity programs. Even so, there is considerable discretionary authority left to the Secretary of Agriculture and the administering agencies. In some cases, this discretion may be broad enough to enable administators to change the programs significantly from the original intent of Congress. For example, the Payment-in-Kind (PIK) program of 1983 was not specifically authorized by the 1981 Act but was implemented using the discretionary authority in that bill and older permanent acts. Because of this wide administrative latitude, projections of sector performance and of the cost and effectiveness of alternative programs depend heavily on assumptions about how programs will be managed from year to year.

In many cases, the law establishes only minimum levels for the most important program instruments (for example, nonrecourse loans and target prices), giving the Secretary authority to set them higher if warranted. In times of surplus production and tight budgets, most Administrations attempt to hold down costs by setting the price supports at or near the minima.

Administrative discretion also is extremely important for the operation of supply control programs. While the law authorizes these programs, it usually is left to the Secretary to determine when, in what form, and how extensively they will be used. Those decisions involve requiring that acreage be voluntarily set aside (as a condition of eligibility for loans and price deficiency payments), providing direct payments for land diversion, or using some mix of the two. In addition, the payment rates are left to Secretarial discretion.

Such decisions are almost always difficult. To facilitate producer planning and increase the effectiveness of the programs, the law requires that most program announcements be made long before crops are planted (in the summer for fall-sown crops and in the early fall for spring-planted crops). However, this is far in advance of any concrete evidence about actual supply

167

or demand conditions. Thus, critical decisions for the coming year must be made well before the amount actually produced in the current year is known, or what the demand is likely to be.

In general, the Administration must decide for each crop:

- Whether price support loan and price deficiency payments will be at the legal minimum or higher.
- Whether a land diversion program will be offered, and, if so, how large it is to be for each crop; the size of the voluntary and paid diversion programs; the payment rate per acre if paid diversion is used; and the requirements for diverted land—for example, whether the land must be planted to a cover crop, whether a cost-share payment is to be made for that cover crop, and whether haying and grazing are allowed.
- Operating rules for the loan program, primarily the interest rate to be charged, the length of the loan, and whether the loan may be extended.
- Operating rules for the farmer-owned reserve (FOR): the interest rates; storage payment rates; when entry is allowed—for example, whether grain can enter the reserve at harvest time or only after a regular CCC loan matures; whether a special reserve loan is to be offered; and entry and release rules—for example, market prices that permit sale of reserve grain without penalty.
- CCC sales policies, that is, conditions under which CCC owned commodities can be resold in the commercial market.

An example of the variety of program decisions in recent years is given in Table 1, which lists by year program provisions for corn.

Table 1.
Corn Program Requirements

Year	Voluntary Set-Aside %	mil acres	Paid Diversion %	mil acres	Payment in Kind %	mil acres	Farmer-Owned Reserve $/bu	mil bu	CCC Loans $/bu	mil bu
1980/81	None	None	None	None	None	None	2.40	185	2.25	238
1981/82	None	None	None	None	None	None	2.55	1,310	2.40	302
1982/83	10	2.1	None	None	None	None	2.90	1,166	2.55	1,150
1983/84	10	4.4	10	5.8	10.3	21.5	2.65	425	2.65	201
1984/85	10	4.2	None	None	None	None	2.55	440	2.55	210

The use of discretionary authority is always a highly charged political issue. Typically, farm groups and some segments of the Congress will pressure the Administration to make the programs more lucrative. But other parts of the Administration, notably OMB, will exert pressure to use the programs sparingly and thus hold down costs. The inevitable compromise seldom pleases anyone.

The interaction between external events and administrative decisions over the past four years provides an interesting case study in the use—and consequences—of discretionary authority. The Reagan Administration has been harshly criticized in some quarters for its management of the commodity programs. It has been charged with using them ineffectively because of fundamental philosophical objections to them on the part of key officials, allowing conditions to deteriorate seriously, and then overreacting with drastic actions. The PIK program was characterized as extreme because it was so large that it adversely affected many segments of the industry and was extremely costly to taxpayers, yet produced little permanent improvement.

The situation that led to PIK was several years in the making. During 1980, special rules to alleviate the impact of the Russian grain embargo had caused large amounts of corn to move into reserve. However, the reduced yields and strong markets of that year brought most of that grain back into commercial channels. In 1980/81 and 1981/82, no acreage reduction programs were used and crops were large. Stocks in both the FOR and CCC increased. In 1982/83, a 10 percent voluntary program was implemented but participation was small (only 29 percent of the corn acreage was enrolled in the program). Crops were large and stocks increased still further. The Administration was urged to use stronger supply control programs but steadfastly refused, citing budgetary constraints.

Then, in a sudden turnabout, the PIK program was implemented in 1983/84 with highly lucrative payment rates. Seventy-two percent of the corn area was enrolled, with 31.3 million acres idled. Some 77 million acres were idled for all crops that year. The program requirements for PIK, the most elaborate in many years, are shown in Table 2.

The impact of the program was much more pronounced than expected, in part because of the onset of unanticipated drought in the summer. While this boosted the incomes of some crop producers, the rapid runup in grain prices dealt the livestock industry a heavy blow. The adverse impact spread to input supplying industries, rural businesses, exporters, and consumers.

Table 2.
Eligibility Requirements for PIK

Item	Wheat	Corn	Sorghum	Barley and Oats	Upland Cotton	Rice
			- - percent - -			
Base Acreage Farmers Must Idle to be Eligible for PIK....	15	10	10	10	20	15
Additional Base Acreage Farmers May Idle for Cash Payment.	5	10	10	10[1]	5	5
Proportion of Base Acreage Farmers May Contract in PIK[2].	30	30	30	0	30	30
PIK Payment Rates Per Acre (percent of program yield)....	95	80	80	—	80	80

[1] To be eligible for benefits, producers of barley and oats must participate in the ARP and PLD, but they may not participate in PIK.

[2] Farmers participating up to this level were then eligible to offer the remainder of their base acreage (whole farm option) for the program.

For all its faults, the PIK progam did effectively reduce the huge stocks that had accumulated, providing the conditions for improvement in the farm economy. But the Administration has been criticized for not building on these conditions—indeed, for administrative decisions that allowed the situation to deteriorate once again. In the following year, the Administration used only a 10 percent voluntary set-aside with no paid diversion. This proved to be insufficient incentive for broad participation in the program. It did reduce budget exposure, but it did not prevent large production and the rebuilding of huge stocks. Thus, critics argue that any longer-term benefits PIK might have produced have been negated. Just one crop year after PIK and all its costs, the 1985 season began with huge stocks on hand, low prices, and continued recession in the farm economy.

General References

Martin Abel and Lynn Daft, "Future Directions for U.S. Agriculture Policy." Curry Foundation, 1984.

American Enterprise Institute, "Agricultural Policy in 1985 and Beyond." Panel discussion, January 28, 1985.

American Farmland Trust, *Future Policy Directions for American Agriculture*, 1984.

Center for National Policy, *Food and Agriculture Policies: Proposals for Change*, 1984.

Congressional Budget Office, "Crop Price-Support Programs: Policy Options for Contemporary Agriculture," February 1984.

Curry Foundation. *Agriculture, Stability and Growth: Toward a Cooperative Approach*, 1984.

Jimmye S. Hillman (ed.), *United States Agricultural Policies for 1985 and Beyond*. University of Arizona and Resources for the Future, 1984.

Ronald D. Knutson, J. B. Penn, and William T. Boehm, *Agricultural and Food Policy*. Prentice-Hall, 1983.

S. R. Johnson, Abner W. Womack, William H. Meyers, Robert E. Young II and Jon Brandt, "Options for the 1985 Farm Bill: An Analysis and Evaluation." Food and Agricultural Policy Research Institute, University of Missouri-Columbia/Iowa State University, 1985.

National Agricultural Forum, *Alternatives for U.S. Food and Agricultural Policy*, 1985.

National Governors' Association, "A National Farm Program: Opportunity or Impossibility?," 1984.

Office of Technology Assessment, Congress of the United States. *Technology, Public Policy, and the Changing Structure of American Agriculture: A Special Report for the 1985 Farm Bill*, 1985.

171

Gordon C. Rausser and Kenneth R. Farrell (eds.), *Alternative Agricultural and Food Policies and the 1985 Farm Bill*. Giannini Foundation of Agricultural Economics, University of California, 1984.

Gordon C. Rausser and William E. Foster, "Agricultural Policy: A Synthesis of Major Studies and Options for 1985." National Center for Food and Agricultural Policy and the National Agriculture Forum, 1984.

United States Department of Agriculture, *A Time to Choose: Summary Report on the Structure of Agriculture,* January 1981.